How To Draw
THE FIGURE

JAMES HORTON

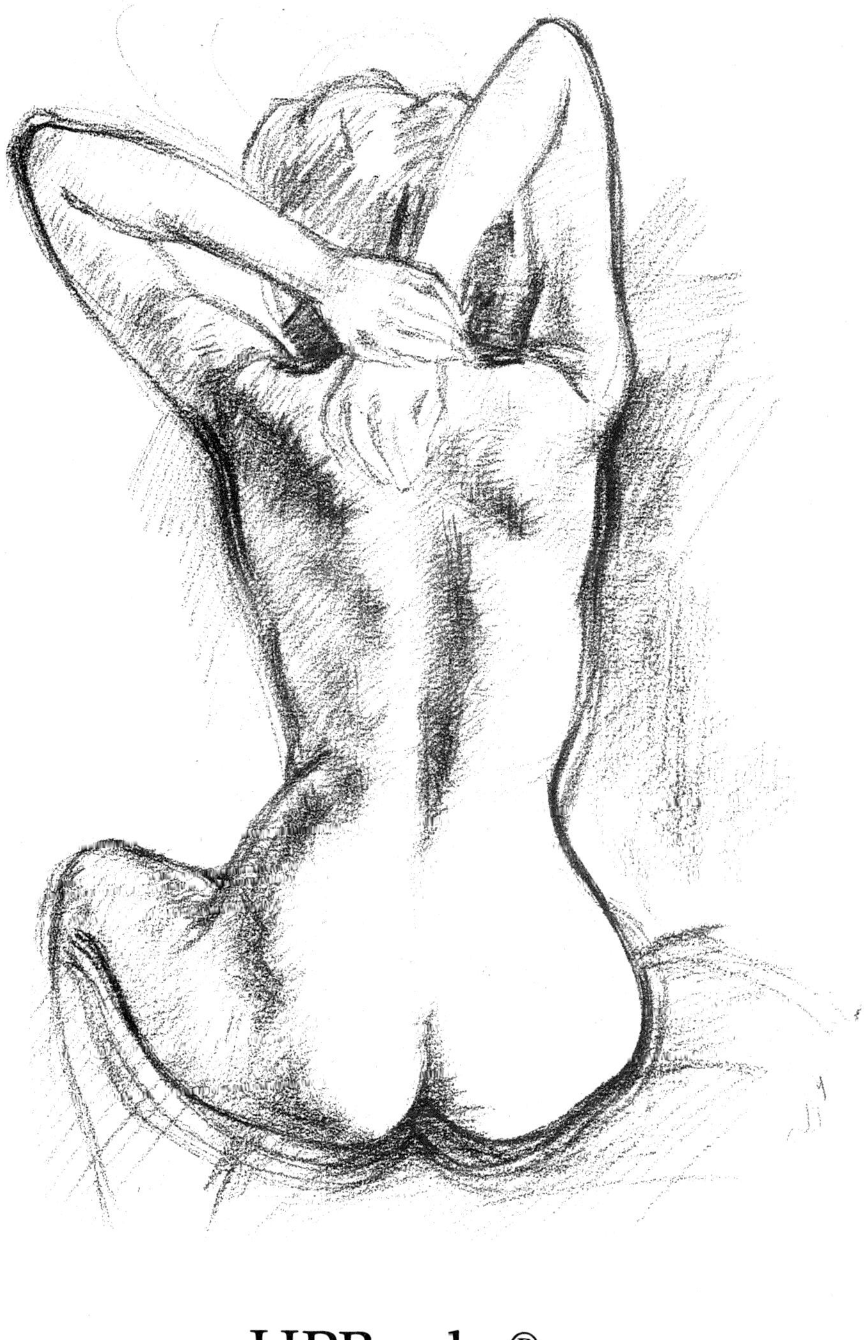

HPBooks®

Published in the United States by
HPBooks, Inc.
P.O. Box 5367
Tucson, AZ 85703
602/888-2150
Publisher: Rick Bailey
Editorial Director: Randy Summerlin
Editor: Melanie Livingston
Art Director: Don Burton
Book Assembly: Leslie Sinclair
Typesetting: Cindy Coatsworth, Michelle Carter
Book Manufacture: Anthony Narducci
Consultants: Posner's Art Store, Stuart Brown,
Ed Mendelson

Printed in the U.S.A.
1st Printing

First published in 1985 by
Collins Publishers, Glasgow and London

ISBN: 0-89586-421-5
Library of Congress Catalog Card Number: 85-60747

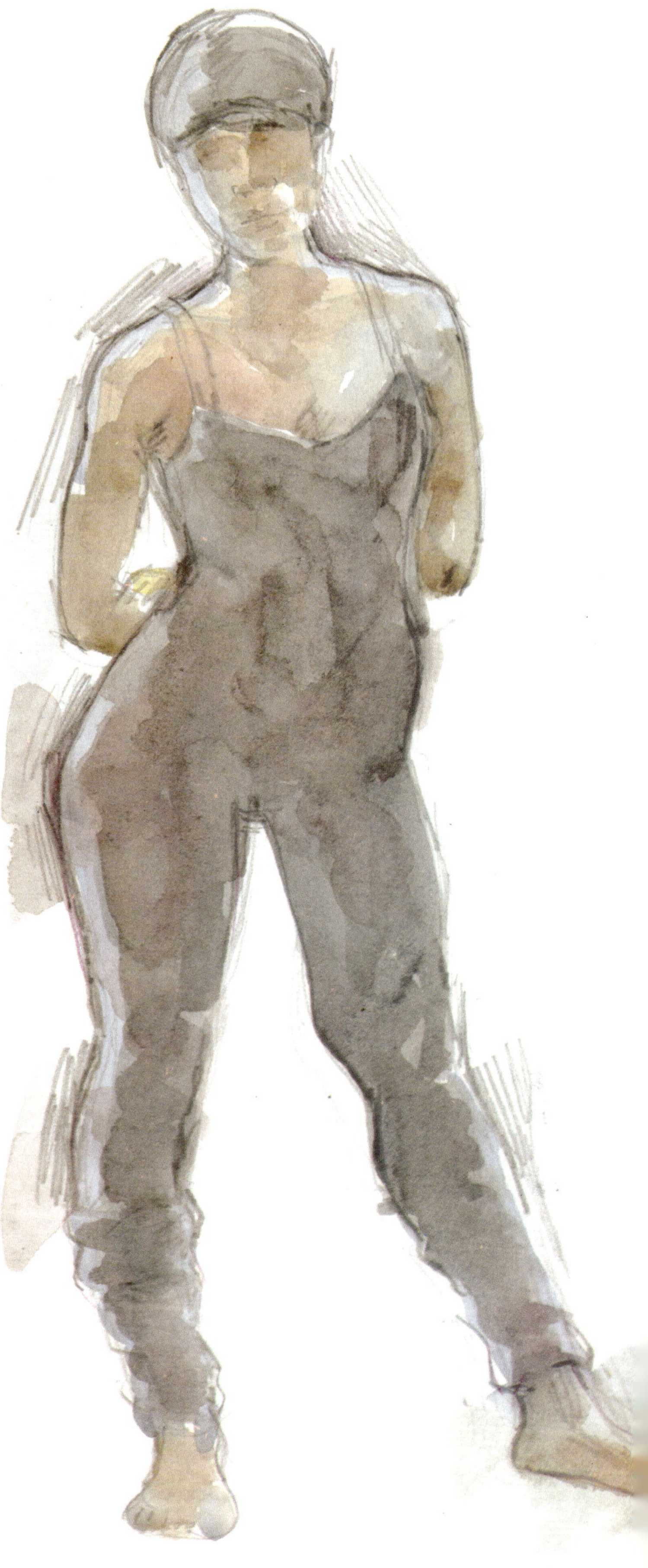

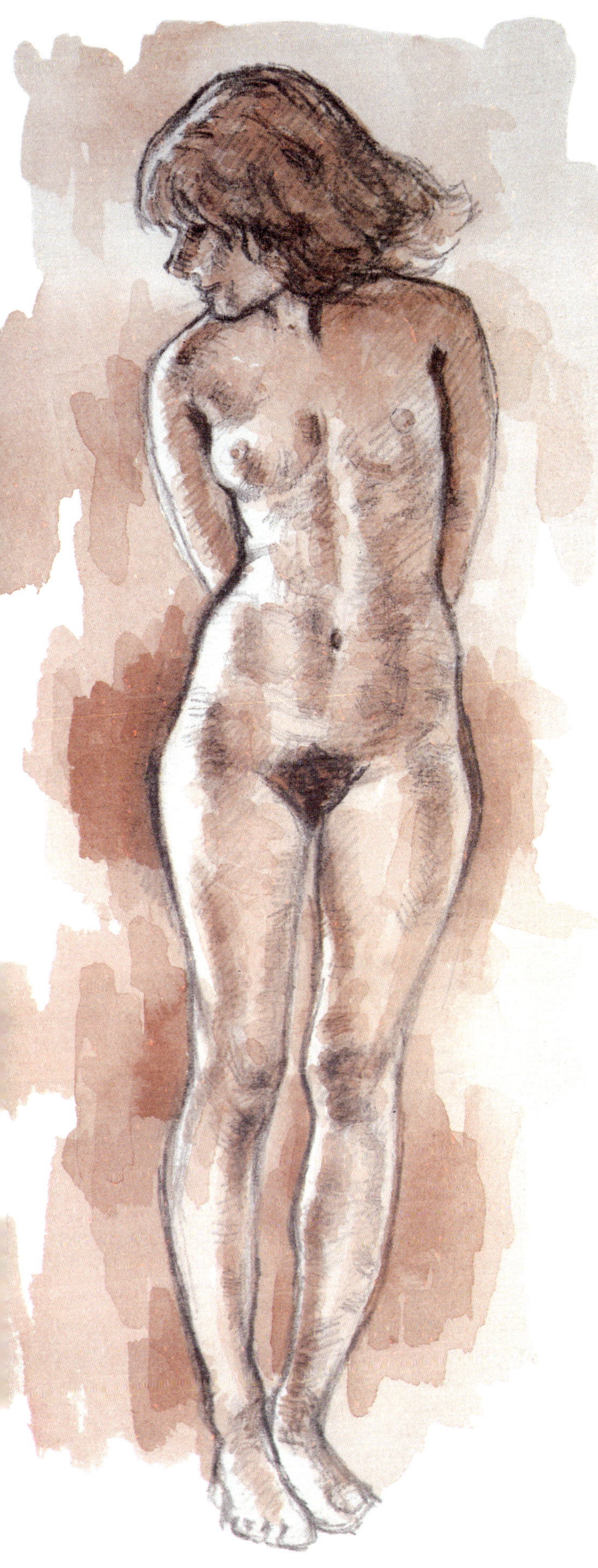

CONTENTS

Portrait Of An Artist

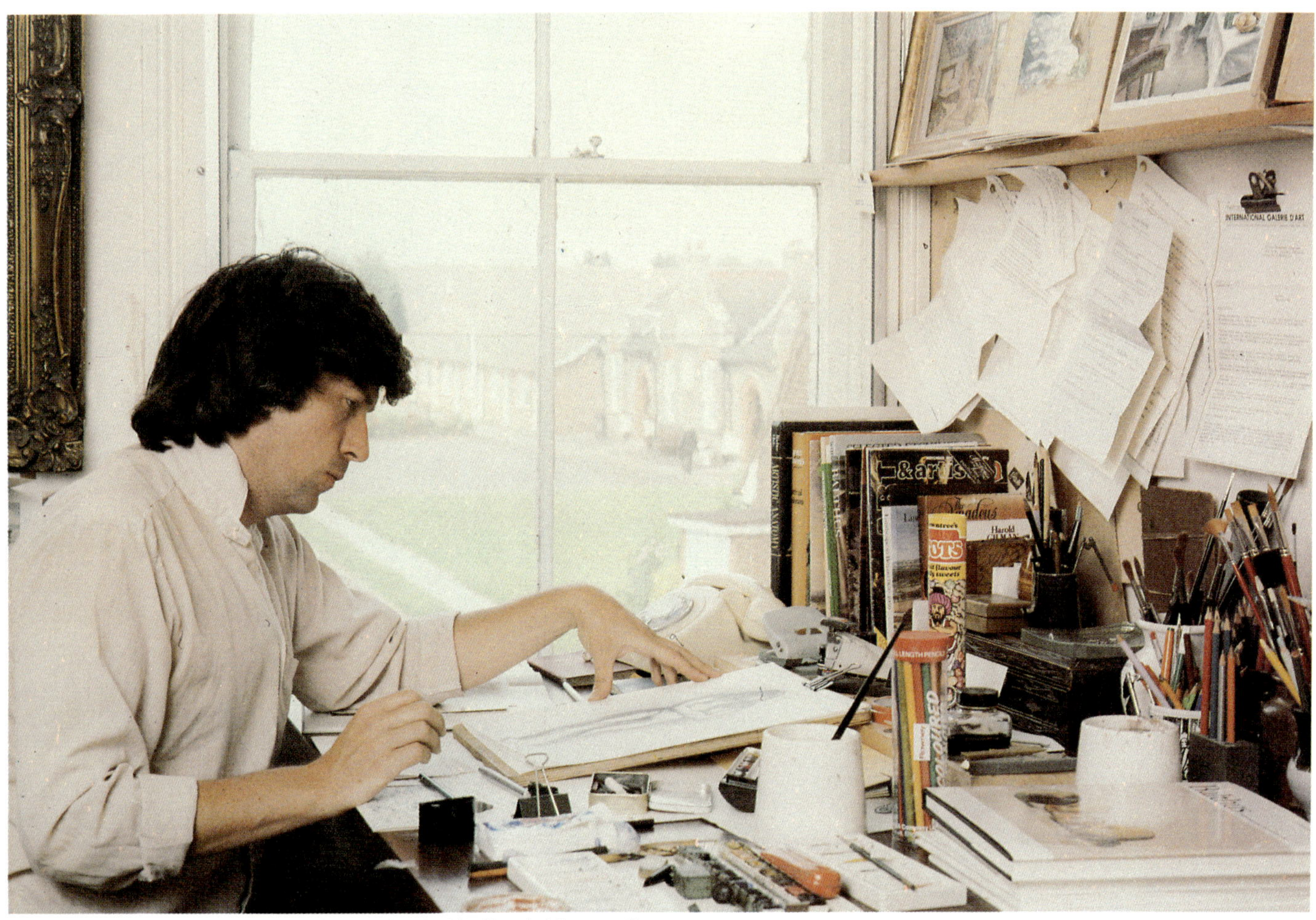

James Horton at work on a pencil drawing in his Cambridge studio.

James Horton was born and educated in London, England. His father was a stonemason who worked in marble and granite, but who was also interested in painting and drawing. This sparked James's original desire to be an artist. James was in his early teens when he first seriously considered a career in art. At 16, he felt confident enough in his artistic abilities to leave his regular school and enter art school.

He studied drawing and painting for two years with Percy Horton, whose love and understanding of great drawings strongly influenced James' art and character. For the next four years he continued his studies at a small art school that emphasized figurative techniques. During this period James Horton also worked a great deal on figurative sculpture. He was then awarded a scholarship to study Renaissance painters and sculptors in Florence, Italy.

Horton spent the next three years at the Royal College of Art in London. His work was included in the Young Contemporaries exhibition, and he won an award from the Institute of Contemporary Art in London. Since leaving the Royal College, Horton has exhibited widely, in England as well as in various European capitals. In 1980 he was elected to the Royal Society of British Artists.

James Horton's works vary in size from small landscapes or figure studies to large figurative paint-

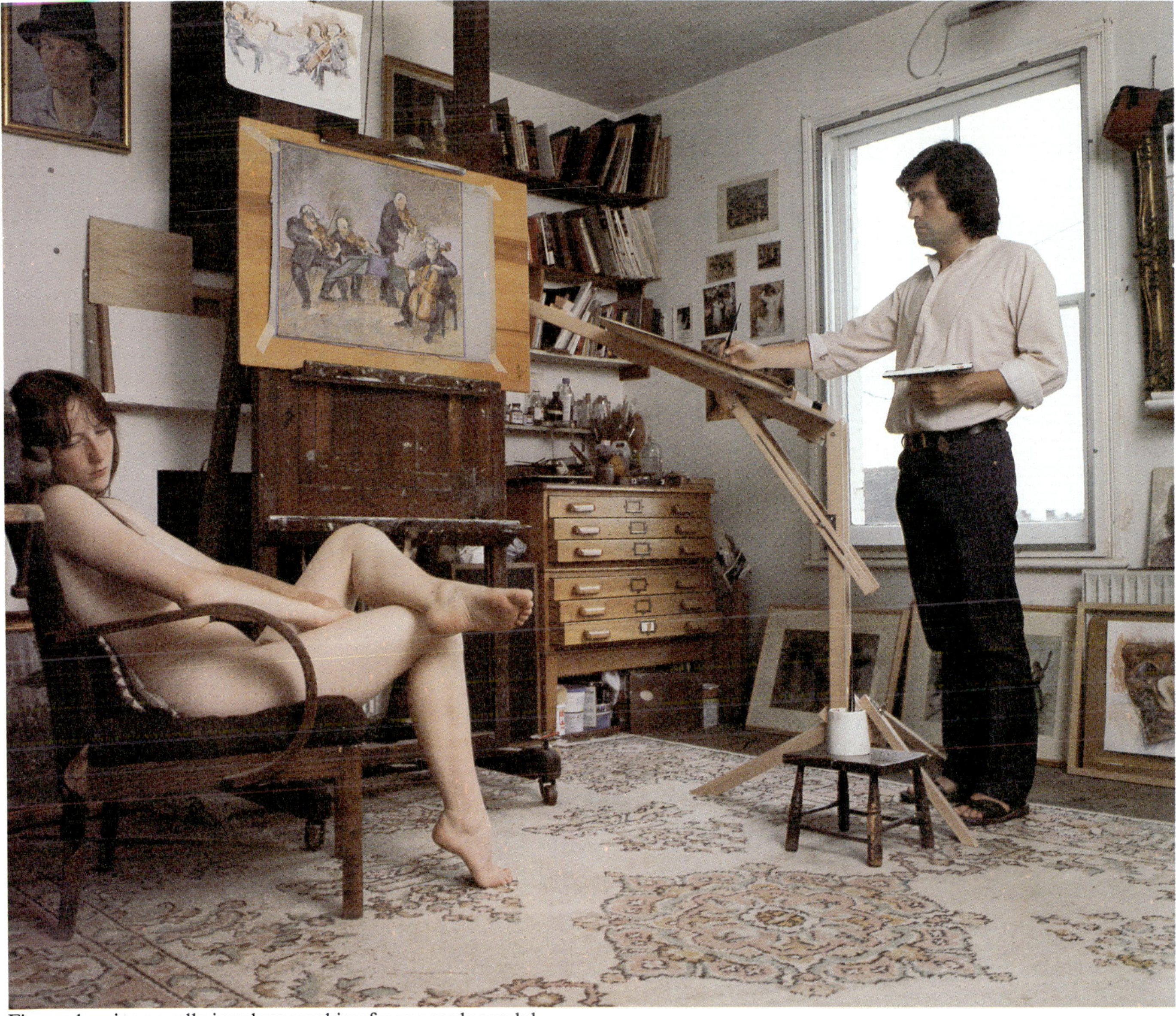

Figure drawing usually involves working from a nude model.

ings that take months to plan and execute.

In addition to drawing and painting, Horton regularly publishes articles on art. He is also an accomplished musician, and has taught and given performances in classical guitar.

James Horton is now a known and respected teacher of art, whose students provide him with inspiration for his own work. He lives and teaches in Cambridge and is also a visiting lecturer at various London art schools.

Equipment

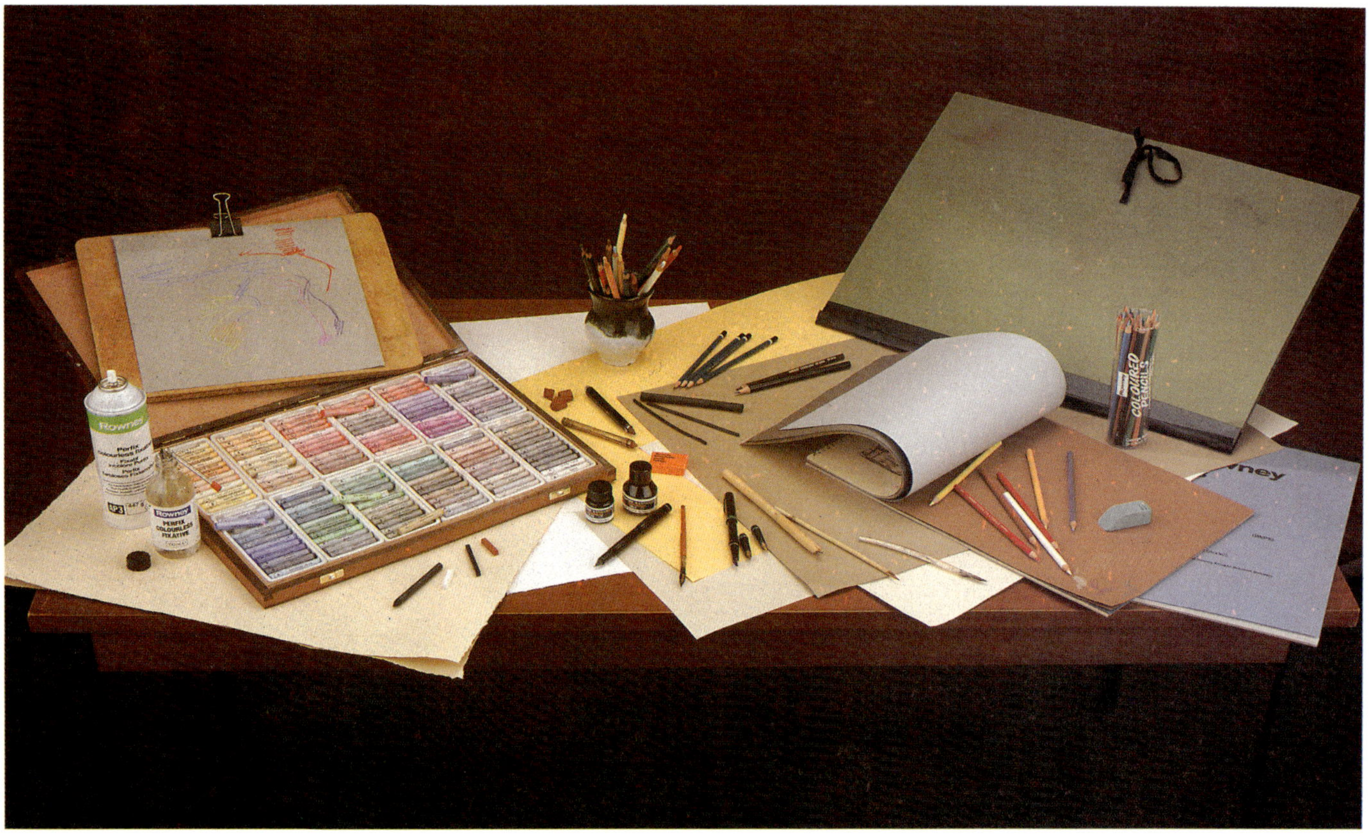

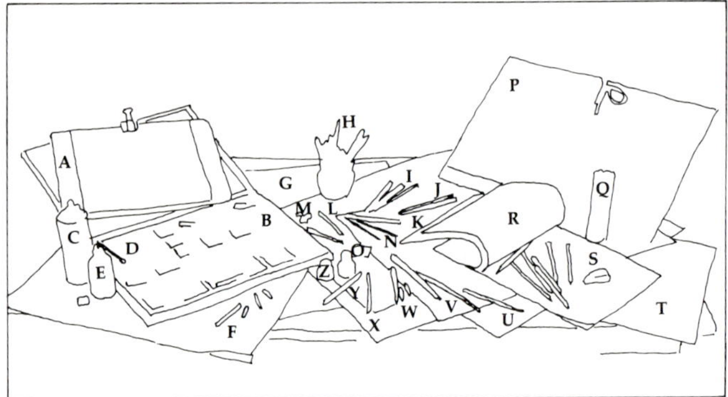

Equipment for drawing with pastels, chalks, pencil, charcoal, colored pencil, and pen and ink:

A) Small drawing board
B) Box of soft pastels
C) Aerosol fixative
D) Fixative spray nozzle
E) Spray fixative
F) Conté processed chalks
G) Assorted papers
H) Pastel pencils
I) Graphite pencils
J) Charcoal pencil
K) General purpose pencil
L) Processed-chalk holder
M) Sanguine chalk with holder
N) Charcoal sticks
O) Putty eraser
P) Portfolio case
Q) Colored pencils
R) Pad of Ingres rag paper
S) Gum eraser
T) Sketchbook
U) Quill pen
V) Reed pens
W) Technical drawing pen with detachable nibs
X) Dip pen
Y) Technical drawing pen
Z) Drawing inks

To make a drawing you need only a pencil and a sheet of paper. However, this is a limiting combination. Sooner or later, you'll want to experiment with different types of media.

Looking at the photo above, you might conclude that an enormous amount of equipment is required. Although some of this is necessary to begin work, if you are just learning to draw, you will not need all of these items. For now, you should invest only in the medium you find most appealing.

QUALITY

The question of quality is always a difficult one. Professional artists need to use the best-quality equipment available. But it is up to you to acquire the materials you can afford. For beginners, the cheapest range of materials is usually adequate.

Most *oil, acrylic* and *watercolor* paints come in two basic categories. *Student-quality* paints have certain additives to "stretch" the color. They are not as permanent as higher-grade paints. *Artist-quality* paints are made with the best raw materials. Of course, the difference is reflected in the price.

You will also notice a difference in the *handling quality* of the various grades of materials. For instance, sable brushes perform better than synthet-

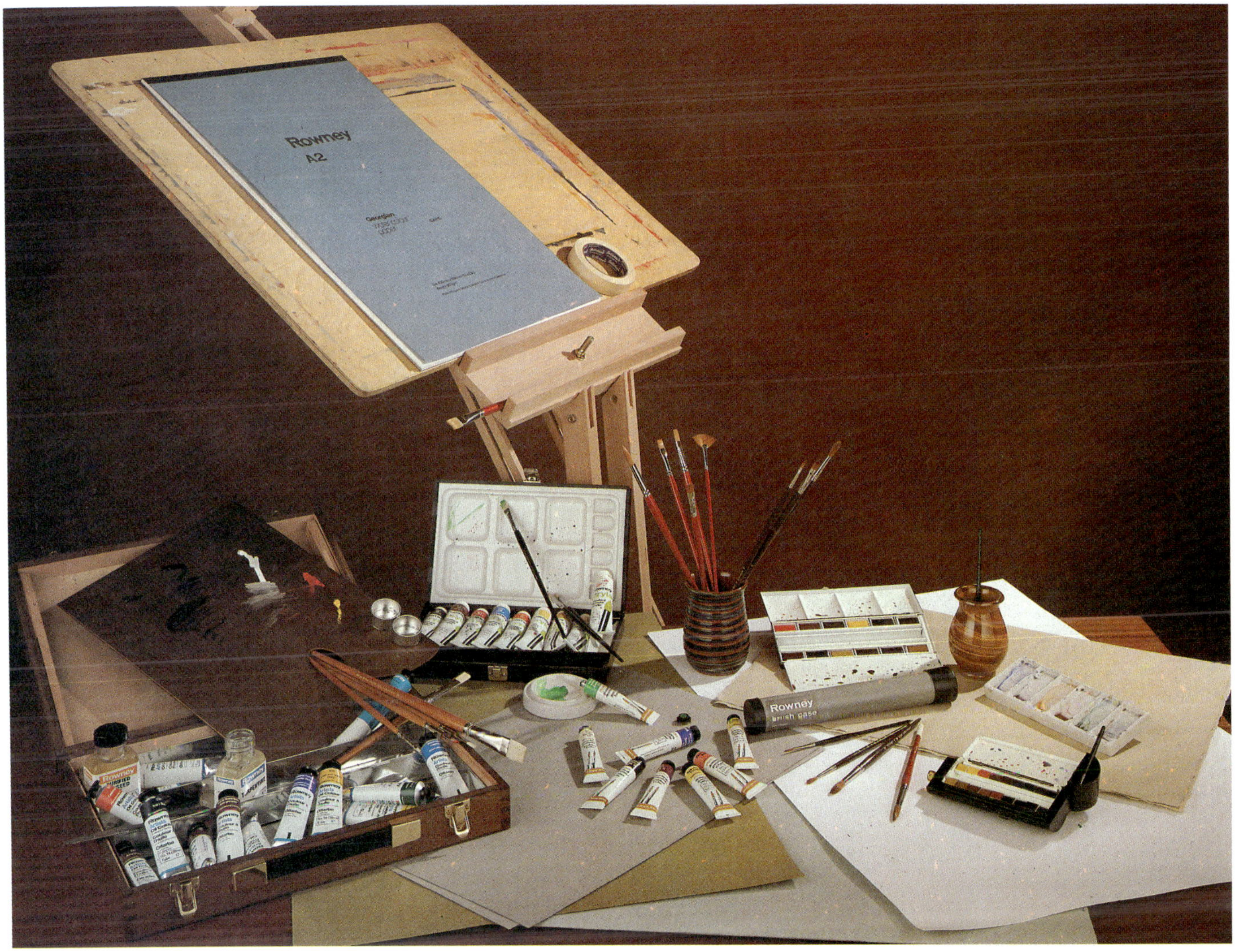

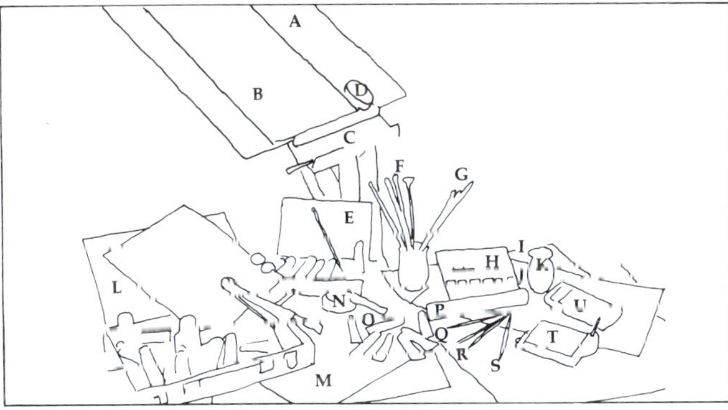

Equipment for drawing with acrylic, watercolor, oil and gouache:

A) Large drawing board
B) Large watercolor pad
C) Easel
D) Masking tape
E) Acrylic paint box
F) Nylon brushes
G) Sable brushes
H) Studio watercolor box
I) Heavy watercolor paper
J) Hand-made watercolor paper
K) Water pot
L) Basic oil-painting set
M) Selection of colored papers
N) China paint well
O) Gouache paints
P) Brush case
Q) Best-quality sable watercolor brush
R) Cheaper sable brushes
S) Nylon watercolor brush
T) Small portable watercolor box
U) Large china paint well

ic ones. Artist-quality colors are more vivid than student-quality colors. Cheap grades of paper will eventually turn yellow and brittle. It may take you some time to acquire professional-quality materials, but this is a good goal to keep in mind.

BASIC EQUIPMENT

If you're considering investing in some drawing equipment, the following items should be on your list.

Easel—One of the most basic pieces of equipment is an easel. You can manage without an easel by propping a sketchbook or a board on your knees, but this can get uncomfortable. The easel in the picture above is sturdy and can hold a large drawing board.

Watercolor Boxes—It's a good idea to have two watercolor boxes. The small, portable box illustrated above can be carried in a pocket. It has a water pot attached, making it convenient for working outdoors.

The bigger watercolor box is designed for more involved work. You can use it, along with the *china paint wells,* to mix larger *washes.* You may fill a watercolor box with the colors you choose, but as a beginner you should use the ready-made versions instead. These come with an adequate selection of colors.

Brushes—Watercolor brushes do not have to be expensive. *Sable* brushes are the best—but they aren't cheap. *Synthetic* imitations are an excellent alternative for both amateur and professional painters. Some manufacturers now make brushes that are part sable and part nylon. These are more affordable than pure sable brushes, but perform almost as well.

If you choose to buy a sable brush, one medium- to large-size brush should be sufficient. If the sable brush is not within your price range, I suggest that you substitute three synthetic brushes, preferably sizes 2, 6 and 11.

Brush Care—No matter how much you pay for your brushes, it is essential to care for them properly. Never push down hard on a brush when rinsing it—this can damage the hairs. Never let paint dry on the brush, especially acrylic or oil paint. Clean the paint from the brushes with the proper solvent.

The best way to care for your brushes is to keep them in a *brush case* when they are not in use.

Oil Painting Equipment—The oil paint box shown on page 7 is a standard set. This includes brushes, a *palette,* and a basic range of colors. You can buy oil paints separately, but if you're just beginning, a ready-made box such as this one is ideal. You will also need a palette for mixing colors, some *turpentine* and *linseed oil* to mix with the paint, and a *palette knife.* You use the palette knife to remove unwanted paint from either the palette or the painting surface.

Pastels—Pastels also come in a range of standard colors. But unlike other media, pastels are then graded into various *tints.*

Small sets of pastels are available, sometimes with groups of colors put together by the manufacturer for work in portraits, figures or landscape.

Colored Pencils—Like pastels, colored pencils cannot be mixed. But this is not necessarily a drawback. Drawings made with colored pencils usually have a different effect than drawings made with pastels or paints. A set of 24 colored pencils should be sufficient for your purposes.

Pen and Ink—The term *pen and ink* covers a very wide range, especially if we include commercial pens such as *felt-tips. Technical drawing pens,* such as Rapidographs and the like, hold their own ink supply. But with the traditional *dip pens,* such as *quill, reed* and *steel-nib pens,* you need to use open bottles of ink.

Chalk—There are many different colors and grades of chalk available for drawing. *Conté* chalks are popular among artists, and come in white, gray, sepia, black and sanguine colors.

Materials for Erasing and Fixing—You will need a *putty eraser* to remove chalk, charcoal or pastel from your drawings. The putty eraser is a soft, pliable piece of rubber that is formable into any shape. To erase, you lift the unwanted part off the paper by dabbing gently, rather than by rubbing out. You can use an ordinary gum eraser when you are working in pencil.

To prevent flaking or smearing on the surface of a drawing, use chemical *fixative.* It's available in an aerosol can or in a bottle with a spray diffuser.

Paper—The paper used for the work in this book represents only a part of what is available in drawing paper. As a general rule, each paper has a medium to which it is best suited. But each artist, of course, makes his own choices.

Pastel works best on colored paper. The colored paper allows all colors—but primarily light colors—to be seen more easily. This is also true of oil, acrylic and gouache paints.

If you are using oil paints, the paper must be *sized* to prevent the oil from soaking into it. To do this, you apply a glaze made of water and glue, or even a thin layer of matte house paint. This makes the paper less porous. Pre-sized paper is also available, but it is more expensive.

Watercolor paper needs to be *stretched* before you use it. Soak the paper in water for five minutes, then lay it out flat on a board and tape it down with *gumstrip.* You need to wet the gumstrip first to activate the glue. Do not try to stretch your paper using self-adhesive tapes.

As the paper dries it contracts, and any wrinkles will pull tight and disappear. If you're willing to pay a little extra, you can buy *watercolor blocks* with pre-stretched paper.

Colored chalks, in combination with white, can also be used on colored paper. Ink works best on high-quality, heavy writing paper. Colored pencils will work well on any white or cream-colored paper. You can use almost any type of paper—as long as it's not too dark—when you are drawing with ordinary pencil.

Portfolio—The last item you may want to purchase is a *portfolio* case. Use it to protect new paper or to store your finished drawings.

Posing The Model

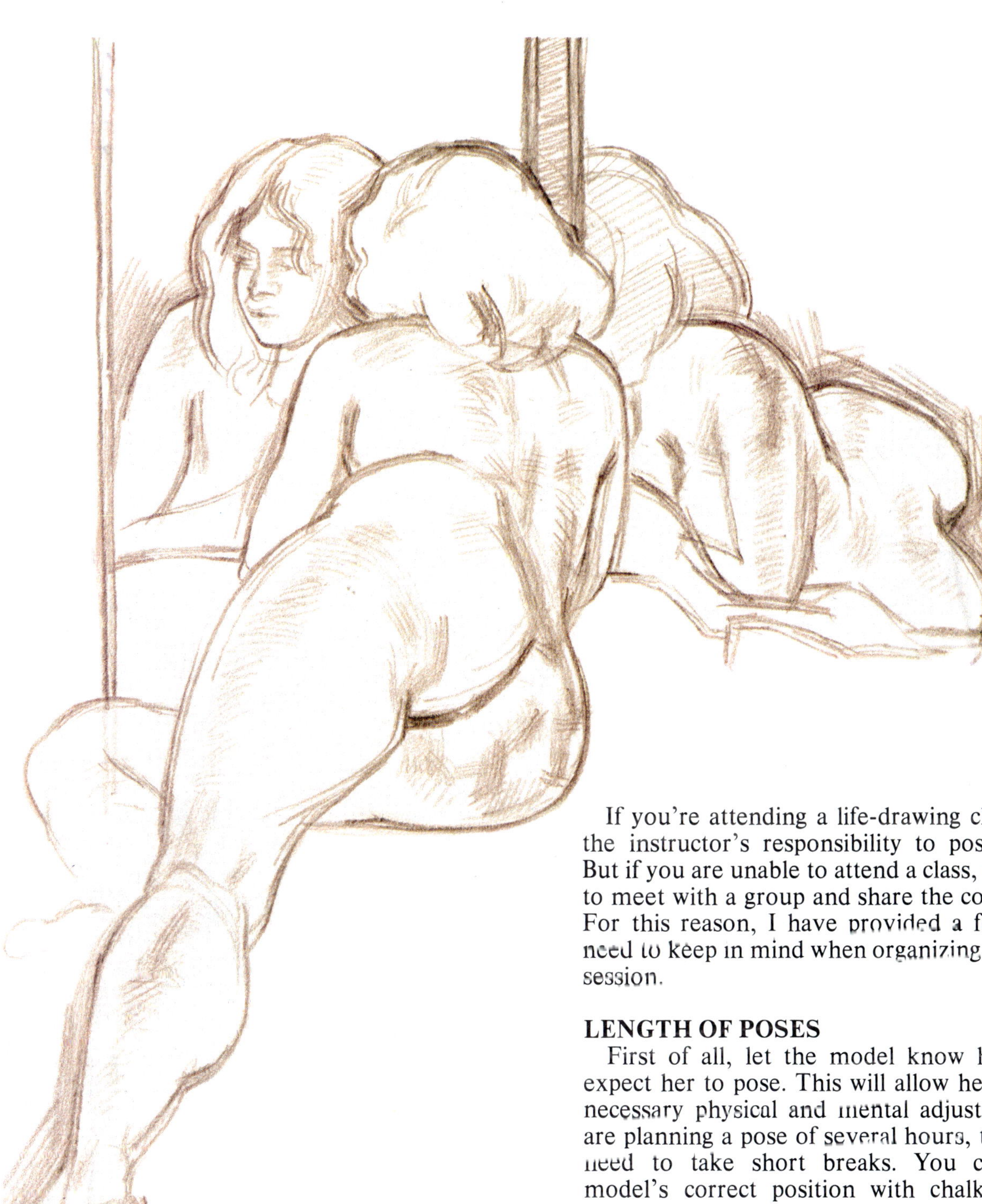

Colored-pencil drawing.

If you're attending a life-drawing class, it will be the instructor's responsibility to pose the model. But if you are unable to attend a class, you may want to meet with a group and share the cost of a model. For this reason, I have provided a few tips you'll need to keep in mind when organizing a life drawing session.

LENGTH OF POSES

First of all, let the model know how long you expect her to pose. This will allow her to make the necessary physical and mental adjustments. If you are planning a pose of several hours, the model will need to take short breaks. You can mark the model's correct position with chalk or strips of masking tape on the floor and surrounding objects.

In general, difficult or dynamic poses will have to be short. The average length of a single stretch for a model is about 45 minutes. The model should never maintain her position for more than an hour without a break. If she is standing or maintaining some other tiring pose, it's best to take a break every 30 minutes or so.

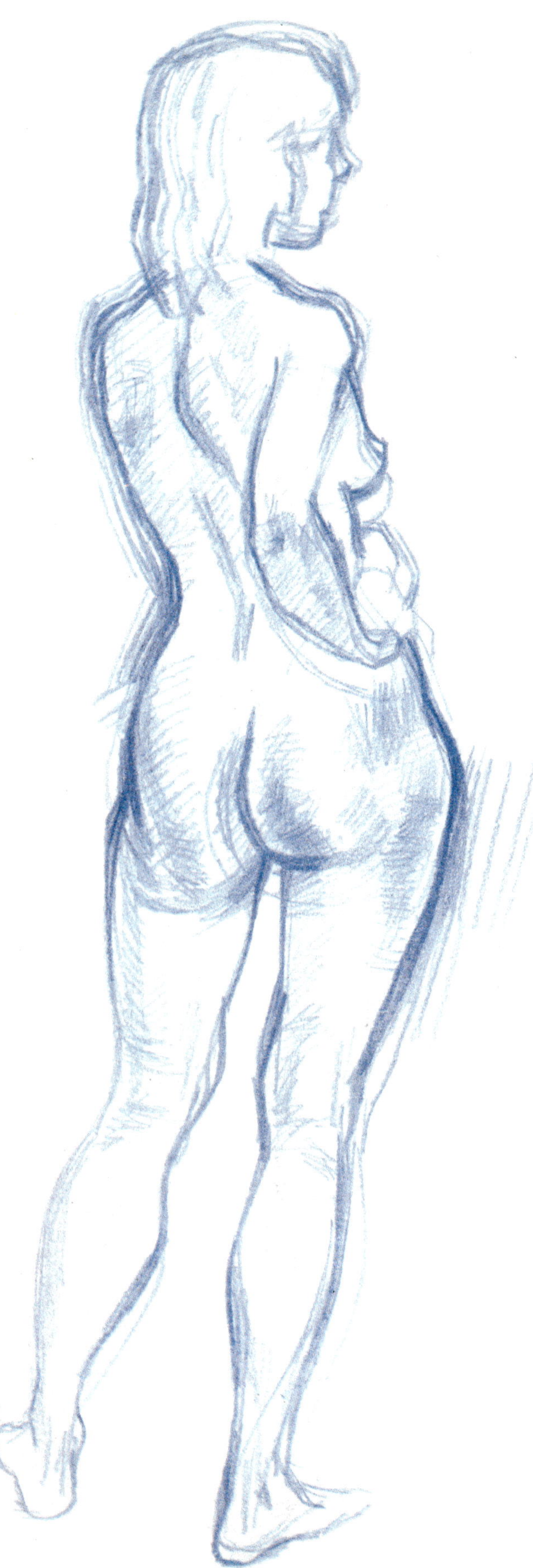

A Word of Caution—If a model says that she is becoming uncomfortable, stop work right away and give her time to rest. I have known models to seem fine one minute and then faint the next!

PROPS

It will help to provide your model with props. You can use a couch, a stool, or anything that will support the figure in a variety of positions. You may also need a set of colored drapes. Use these to make the pose more comfortable for the model, or just to provide some immediate background for the figure.

PREPARING YOURSELF

Once the model is settled, it is the artist's turn to make adjustments. Walk around the model and consider the different possibilities for a drawing that each viewpoint provides. You'll find that some poses look uninteresting from one position and quite fascinating from another. This is largely due to lighting changes. Never accept what happens to be the pose from your initial location. Be selective!

Different eye levels will also affect your perception of the pose. If the model is posed on the floor and you are standing at an easel, interesting downward views may result. Conversely, if the model is posed on a raised platform—as is often the case in life-drawing classes—you will perceive the figure essentially at eye level.

If you are drawing in a small or crowded room, you may have little choice about where you position yourself. In this case, try to learn something from the discipline of coping with a less-than-advantageous perspective.

The Long and the Short of It—Try to vary the length of the poses from session to session. It's especially important to practice drawing poses of 10 minutes or less. Because these short poses require great speed in drawing, they can be disconcerting to inexperienced artists, Nevertheless, this is an important step to master. Later in the book I'll discuss the value of drawing from a moving model. This will be much easier once you feel confident about the swift execution each short pose demands.

Remember that when you draw rapidly, you are not after a finished picture. Rather, you are trying for the image that captures the *essence* of the pose. Perhaps the greatest advantage of the short pose is that you can ask your model to adopt dynamic positions that would be impossible to hold for long periods.

Colored-pencil drawing.

Starting A Drawing

The saying "All beginnings are difficult" is particularly true of beginning a drawing. I feel that the best tactic is the one adopted when going swimming—instead of creeping in an inch at a time, jump in!

But before jumping, you need to consider the length of pose, the size of paper, and the medium you'll use. For example, if you are planning to draw in a small sketchbook, thick charcoal or pastels are probably not a good idea. These media will fill the drawing area too quickly. By the same token, it would take a long time to build up an image on a large sheet of paper with a thin HB pencil.

However, both these combinations are feasible under certain circumstances. You might use the charcoal and small sketchbook for a three-minute *gesture drawing*. Similarly, a pose of several hours could allow the gradual building-up of an image drawn with pencil.

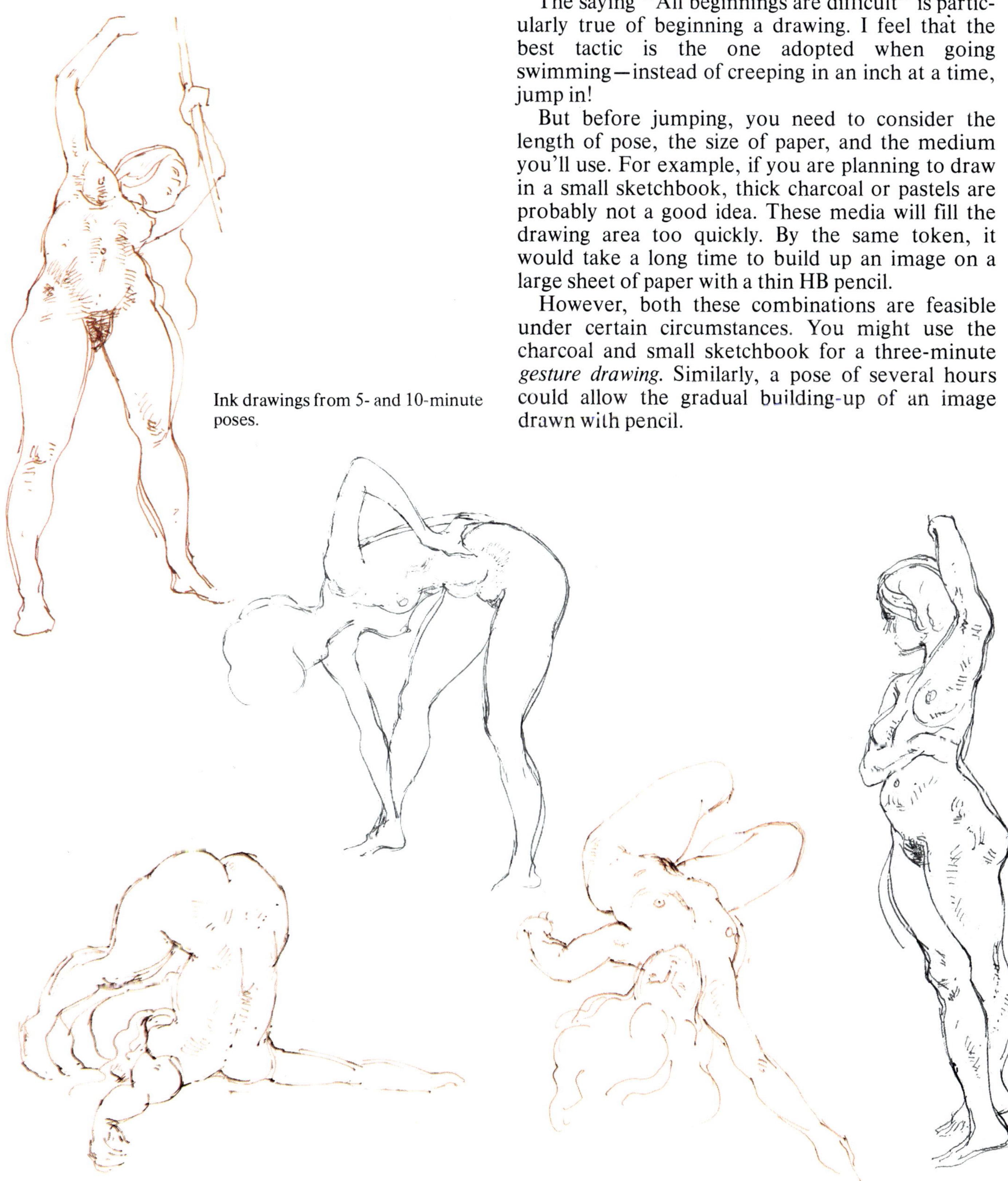

Ink drawings from 5- and 10-minute poses.

You'll also want to consider the *image size*—the size of your drawing on the paper—before you begin. Work out roughly in advance how much of the paper you want the drawing to occupy. Your objective is to draw the figure as a whole, and poor planning can make this difficult.

To get your life-drawing session started, and to overcome a tentative beginning, I suggest you start with a series of 5- and 10-minute poses. You can see some examples of short poses, drawn in ink, on the previous page. Such a time limit forces you to draw quickly and roughly. Soon your adrenaline begins to flow, and you find yourself less inhibited about the results of your efforts.

MEASURING

Measuring is essential at some stage of a drawing. It's a way for you to check the proportions of your figure. But I caution you against measuring too carefully in the initial stages. I always do a substantial amount of drawing before I measure—that way I can check the proportions of one part to another.

Trust Your Eye—It's possible to draw by measuring each time you make a mark, then gradually build up a network of interrelated marks. But measuring then becomes a method of construction rather than a method of checking. This, of course, inhibits the jumping-in approach. Moreover, you could get the proportions of your entire drawing wrong, simply by making a slight miscalculation at the beginning.

It's better to begin by trusting your own eye. If you measure only the larger parts of your figure—such as the distance from the neck to the pubic arch, and the pubic arch to the feet—your drawing will be basically accurate from the start.

Distances to Measure—Figures 1, 3 and 4 on the opposite page show the distances that are useful to measure. They are compared to distances on other parts of the body. The best measurements to use will always depend on the particular pose your model is holding.

For example, in figure 4 the distances from head to shoulder and shoulder to waist are approximately the same. Between the waist and the heel, this same distance will fit about four times. Figures 1 and 3 show more ways you can divide the body at obvious points to make comparisons.

Establishing Verticals and Horizontals—The *plumb line* can be a useful aid in measuring, especially for standing poses. This is the same device builders use on site. Its purpose is to establish a true vertical line. To make your own plumb line, you only need to attach a small weight to a piece of string two or three feet long. When you hold this up to the figure, you can tell which parts of the body correspond to the same vertical line.

It's not as easy to establish a true horizontal line. One way is to hold your pencil at arm's length in front of you, trying to keep it as horizontal as possible. A more accurate way is to sit with your drawing board in front of you and lower your eye to the top of the board. As with the plumb line, the idea is to note which parts of the body correspond to the same horizontal line.

Figures 2 and 5 further illustrate the use of verticals and horizontals when measuring. In figure 2 the knee appears on the same vertical line as the armpit. Figure 5 shows you how useful horizontals can be in making sure your image occupies the correct place in space and perspective. You might easily misjudge the spatial relation of the feet to the head in a reclining pose, unless you learn to make this sort of check.

PROPORTION

You will hear the word *proportion* quite a lot within the context of figure drawing. Generally speaking, it refers to the way various parts of the body, usually the limbs, relate to each other. Proportions differ from one individual to another. This means that the key to capturing the unique character of your figure begins with getting the proportions right.

Use Your Eye—Measuring will help, but you should learn to use your eye to determine rough proportions. This is a good reason for including the whole figure when drawing a standing model—it's difficult to get the width of the figure right without knowing the length. I have often seen students' drawings that are not bad in themselves, but when compared to the model do not have the right proportional characteristics.

EXERCISE

Make a drawing from a three-hour pose, allowing the model to rest periodically. Using a plumb line and a horizontal, carefully plot the parts of the figure that correspond to the true vertical and horizontal lines. For the purposes of this exercise, draw in all construction lines. This way, when the drawing is complete, you will be able to see clearly all the parts of the figure that link up.

You may also want to practice making quick drawings, using relative measurements, as illustrated in figures 1, 3 and 4. As before, include construction lines to help you see which body parts are located on the same vertical and horizontal lines.

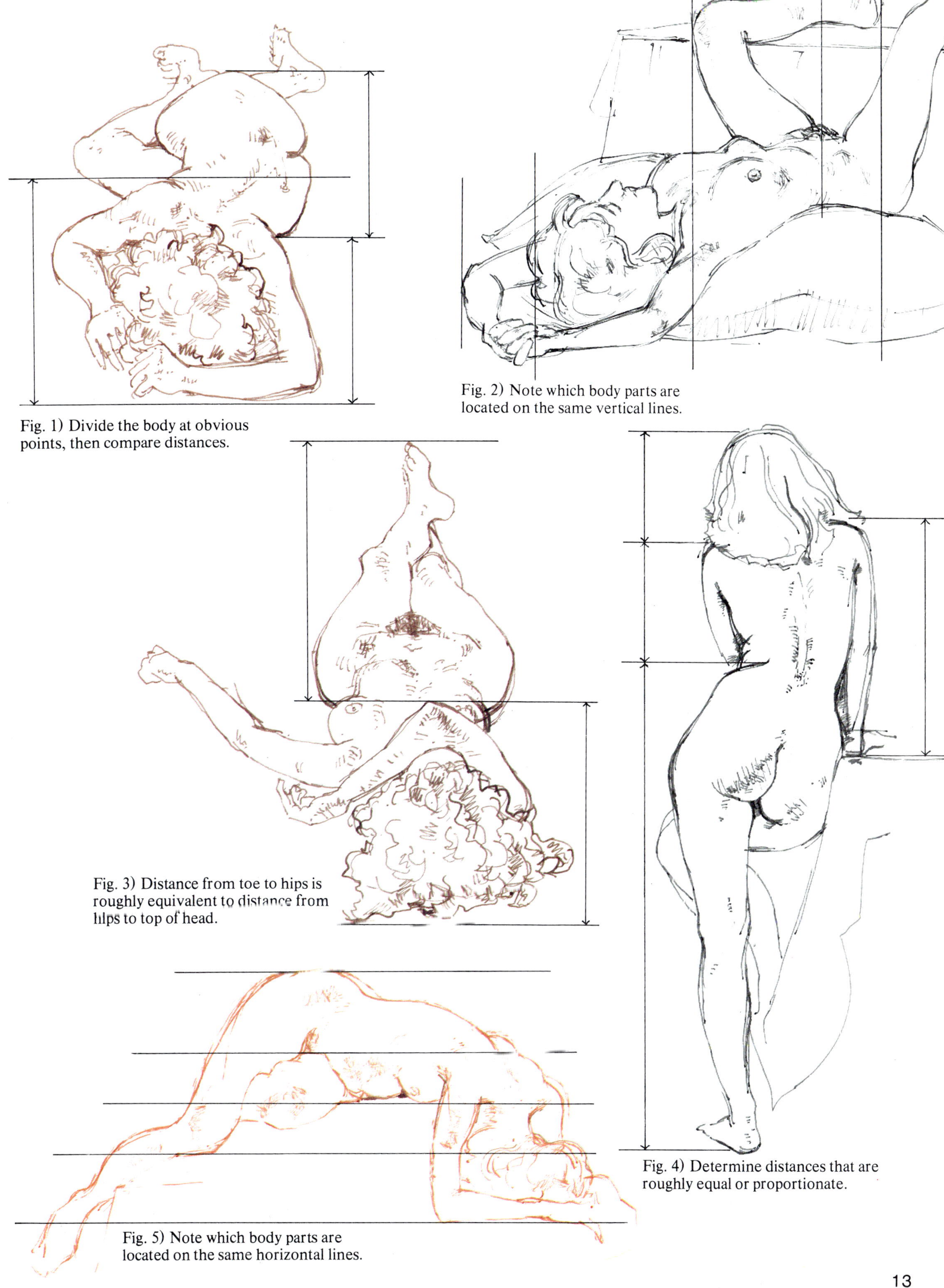

Fig. 1) Divide the body at obvious points, then compare distances.

Fig. 2) Note which body parts are located on the same vertical lines.

Fig. 3) Distance from toe to hips is roughly equivalent to distance from hips to top of head.

Fig. 4) Determine distances that are roughly equal or proportionate.

Fig. 5) Note which body parts are located on the same horizontal lines.

Shape, Form And Balance

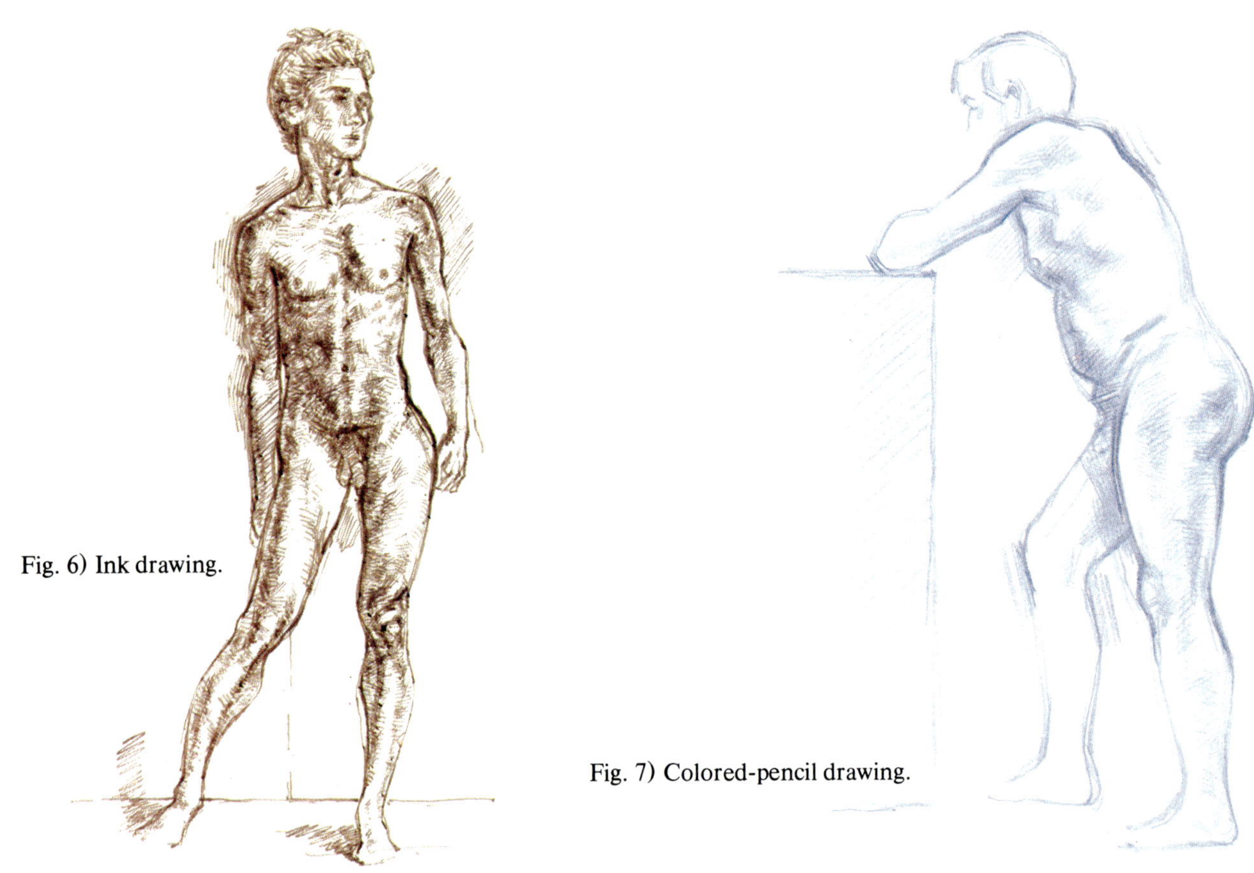

Fig. 6) Ink drawing.

Fig. 7) Colored-pencil drawing.

Now that you know how to begin a figure drawing, you are ready to consider some of the elements involved once the drawing is underway.

SHAPE AND FORM

First, you should look at the shape of your model. Does she resemble the model in figure 8 or the model in figure 10? The shape may seem obvious to you, especially when comparing two such different figures as these.

But inexperienced artists are apt to pay too little attention to the shape of the figure. I have often looked at a selection of drawings made by students in a class, and each drawing seemed to be made from a different model. The point is, it's difficult to achieve the character of a person's shape simply by measuring.

How to Render Shape—Shape and form are elements of drawing that you can tackle in a variety of ways. Your approach will depend on your own goals for a particular drawing and on the character of the model. For instance, in figure 6 above, I found the thin structure of the model's body suitable for making a carefully studied drawing. I wanted to emphasize the precise *changes of plane* and tensions from one part of the body to another. This contrasts sharply with figure 10, where I wanted to capture the round and voluminous quality of the form. Therefore I chose not to make the drawing as intricate.

Figure 7 above has neither generous curves nor sinewy thinness. In this drawing I found it rewarding to express something of the form contained between fairly strong contours. The pose in profile helped to show two sides of the figure relative to one another. In particular, I wanted to show the area between the shoulder blade and the chest, between the stomach and the back, and between the top of the leg and the buttock.

BALANCE

Balance is another important element to consider, especially when you are drawing from a standing pose. Figures 7, 8 and 9 show a variety of ways in which balance can affect a drawing.

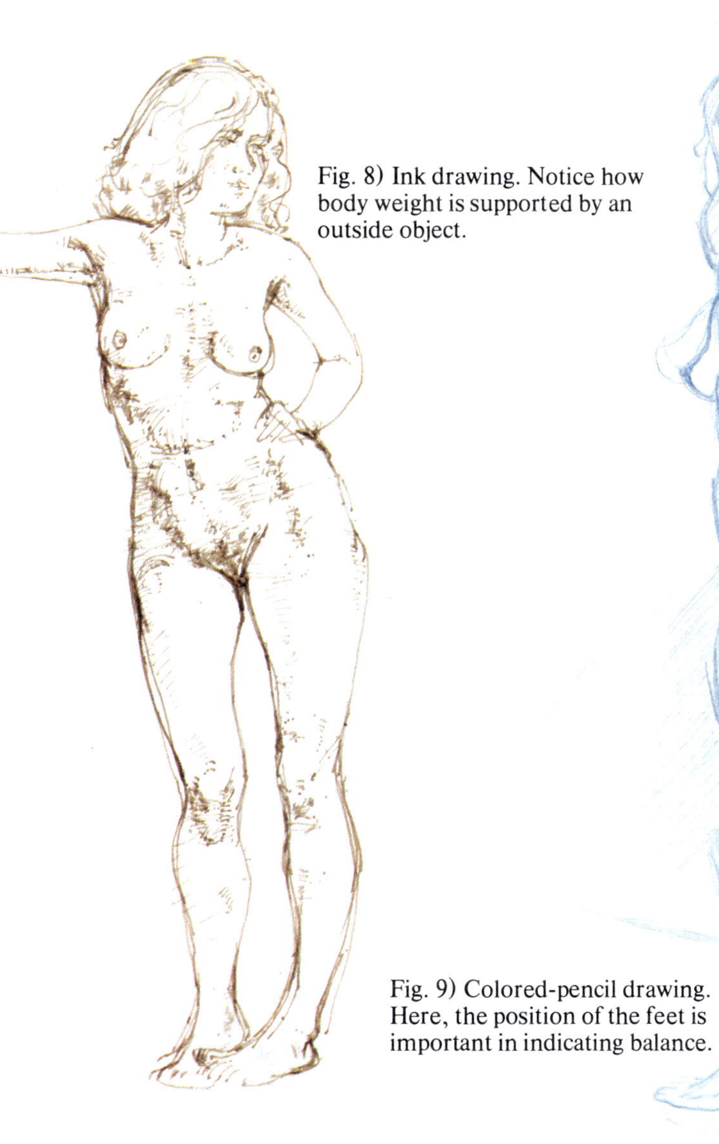

Fig. 8) Ink drawing. Notice how body weight is supported by an outside object.

Fig. 9) Colored-pencil drawing. Here, the position of the feet is important in indicating balance.

Check Angles and Axis—In figure 8, you can see from the angles across the breasts and hips that the weight of the body is supported on some outside object. Notice also the central axis of the torso, which runs between the pit of the neck and the pubic arch. The angle of this axis tells you something about the figure's balance. If the body were supporting its own weight, the mass of the torso would have to rest directly over the weight-bearing leg.

The distance and perspective between the feet in figure 9 also say something about the balance of this stance. If the feet had not been included, the drawing would *never* look properly balanced.

EXERCISE

First, pose the model in a standing position with no outside support, and make a drawing. Then pose the model leaning against a wall or against some other support. Make a second drawing, then observe the differences between the two. Remember to show the central axis of the body by following the line from the pit of the neck to the pubic arch.

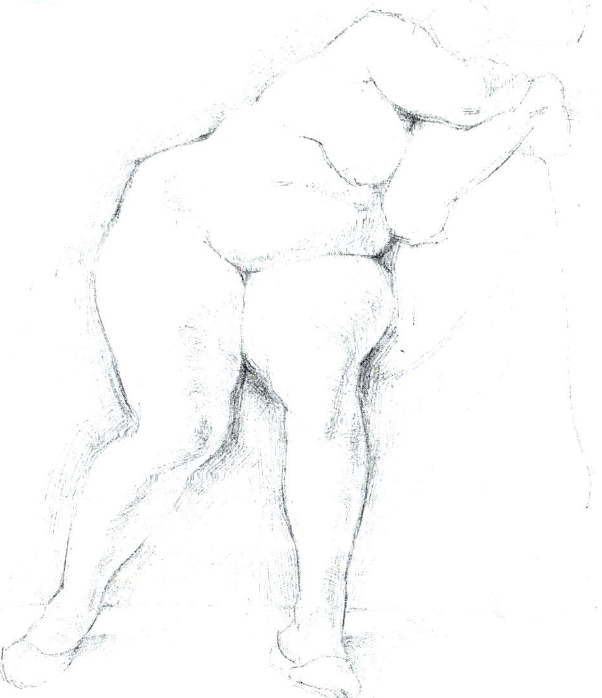

Fig. 10) Pencil drawing.

Tonal Drawing

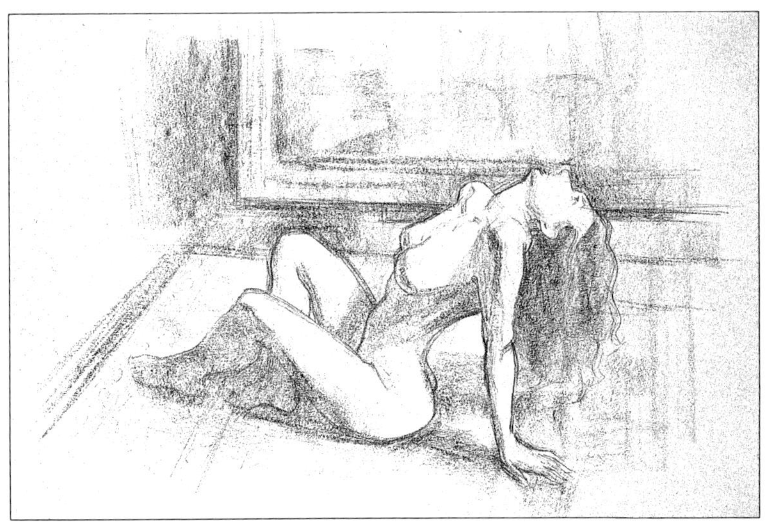

First stage of drawing in black conté chalk.

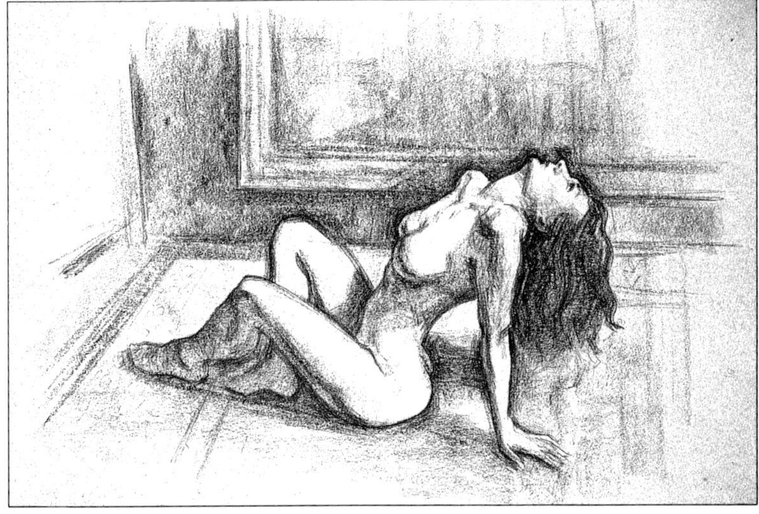

Second stage.

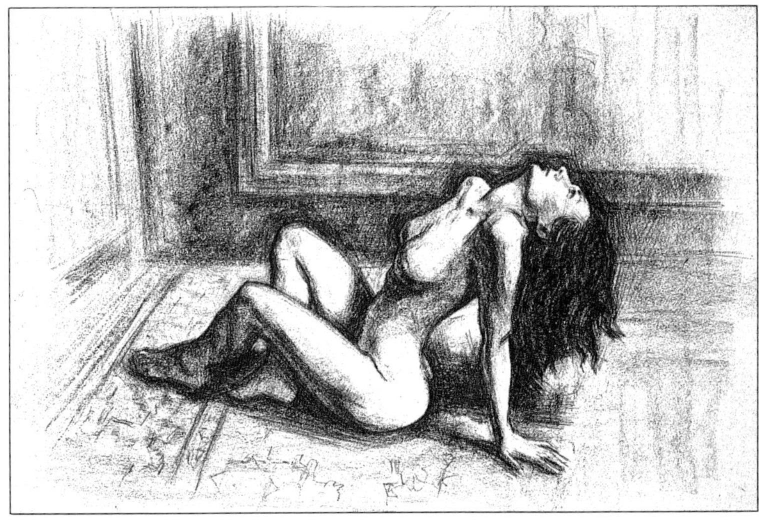

Last stage.

In *tonal drawing* you will use *mass,* or shading, rather than just line. Before you begin a tonal drawing, it is important to select the most suitable light source. A light source that is consistent throughout the pose will work best. Light that comes from a single source is particularly effective, because it will cast clearly defined shadows on the model.

RELATIVE TONES

To gain the most from a tonal drawing, it is essential that you understand *relative tones.* A linear drawing does not need to show background. But for a tonal drawing to be effective, the figure must be seen in relation to its immediate surroundings.

Background Tones—The drawing at right shows a figure standing in light from one source. Notice how the background has been rendered in varying tones. Even though a background may appear uniform on its surface, when an object is placed in front of it, the light falling on that object will make the background vary in tone. These background tonal variations can help give *value* to highlighted parts of the figure.

The background for this drawing was a plain dark cloth. But when the model was placed in front of it, some parts of her immediately looked lighter, while other parts looked darker. In the drawing, much of her left side is actually darker than the background, because it is in full shadow.

Reflected Light—You can also see the effect of reflected light in this drawing. Reflected light usually shows up on a part of the figure nearest the viewer. Here, the right buttock, arm and leg have been highlighted to show the effect of reflected light.

On the previous page you can see the process I went through to make a chalk drawing that would adequately describe form, using only tone.

FIRST STAGE

I began with a very loose linear statement, just to get an idea of where the masses of tone should be. Next, I used the side of the chalk to lightly cover those areas that were at least partially shadowed. You can see that, even at this early stage, a tonal pattern is emerging.

SECOND STAGE

Working another layer on top of the first tone, I strengthened certain areas like the hair and certain parts of the background. To establish a sense of solidity, I also drew in major changes of plane on the figure.

The light for this pose was strong, and came from a single source above the model. This made shadows inevitable. But within the context of a drawing like this, shadows can assist in rendering both form and tonal pattern.

LAST STAGE

The drawing of the figure itself was now well established. I then tried to further enhance the tonal pattern. I worked to develop texture in the hair and in the areas surrounding the face, shoulders, chest and right leg.

EXERCISE

Pose your model in a strong, consistent light source for three hours, taking short breaks as needed. Make a drawing which tries from the outset to describe the subject using only tone. Use the build-up of tonal patterns to construct the drawing. Begin by putting a light tone over all areas not receiving direct light. Then work systematically into that tone, darkening it to indicate areas of greater shadow. Pay special attention to sharp contrasts between light and dark.

Tonal drawing in charcoal, pencil and wash.

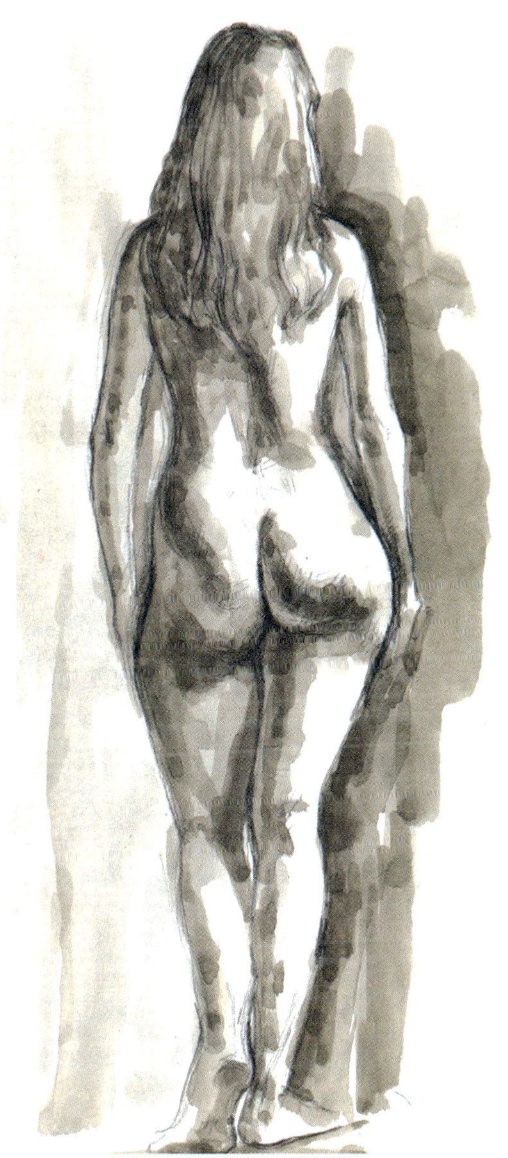

Linear Drawing

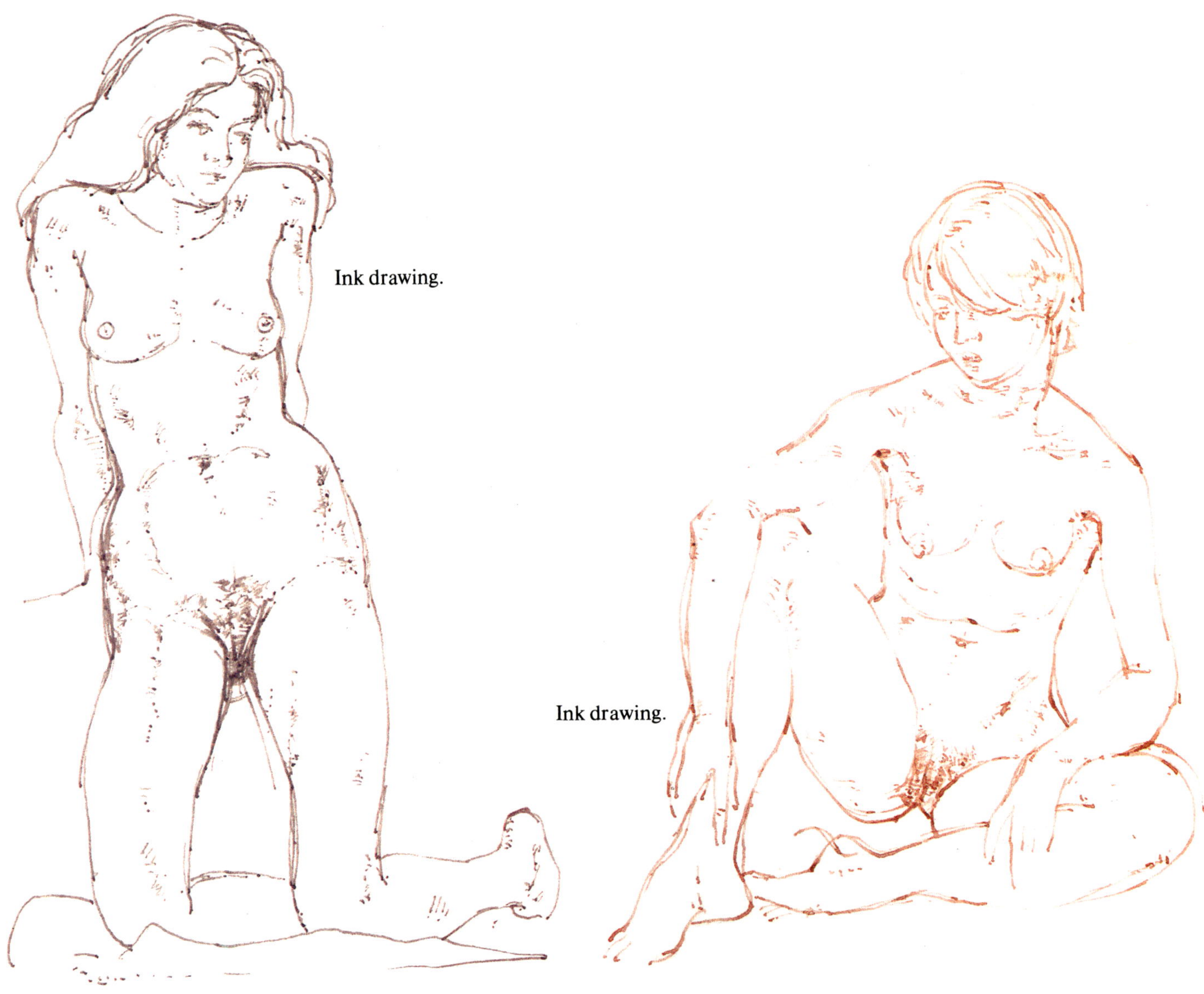

Ink drawing.

Ink drawing.

You probably don't think of types of drawings as fitting neatly into separate categories. However, when learning to draw, it can be beneficial to make distinctions between methods, to understand specific processes. If you look at drawings in museums, galleries or art books, you can often identify a particular approach. For instance, artists like Klimt and Schiele are well known for their linear drawings. Rembrandt, on the other hand, is known for his rich and somber shadows.

I find it very helpful to practice drawing by focusing on one specific method at a time, such as linear or tonal drawing. This forces me to approach a drawing with a singular aim. If you're just learning to draw, I strongly recommend that you practice these methods separately.

In this section you will learn something about the techniques of linear drawing.

A DEFINITION

Linear drawing means, quite simply, expressing ideas with just line, instead of tone or shadow. It does not mean that a drawing should consist of a single line marking the mere contour of a figure.

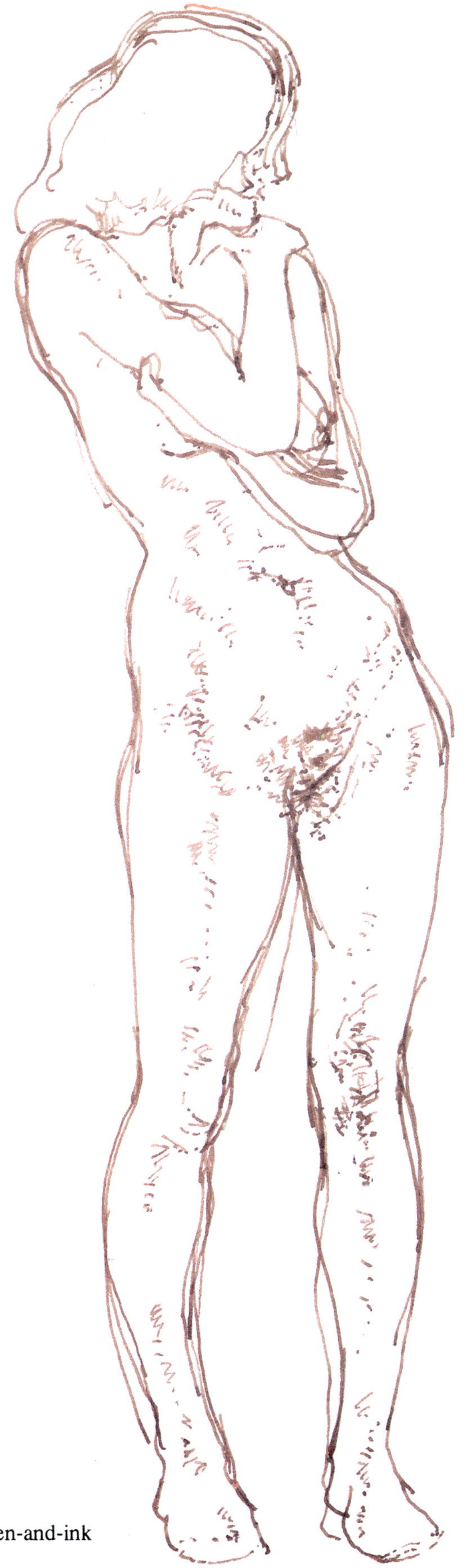
15-minute pen-and-ink drawing.

You can give a linear drawing structure and can indicate shape through changes of plane—as the drawings on page 18 illustrate.

Lighting—Very often, the way you approach a drawing will be determined by the available lighting. It's probably best to try a tonal drawing if the lighting is consistent and comes from a single source. But if the light is diffuse, or comes from more than one source, a linear drawing would be a better choice.

Length of Poses—Another factor in determining what sort of drawing you will make is the planned length of the pose. Relatively short poses, say, of 20 minutes, are ideal for linear drawing. This is because the limited time does not allow for a great deal of overwork. If you make a drawing with a longer pose, you'll be tempted to take it beyond a linear statement by using tone and shadow areas.

What You Need—You can use virtually any medium for a linear drawing. I personally find pen and ink a satisfying combination. The two figures on the opposite page were each drawn in 20 minutes, using a fountain pen and a small sketchbook.

LINE QUALITY

The pen-and-ink drawing on this page was executed in about 15 minutes. You'll see that in addition to the line, I've indicated changes of plane. These additional marks are there merely to give solidity to the figure, and should not distract from or interfere with the flow of the line.

Line quality is fundamentally what this drawing is about. For this reason, I chose not to indicate the direction of the light by shadowing. In several parts of the figure, you can see a single pen line. And even in areas with many lines, such as the top of the head, I was attempting a first-time-right quality. You can achieve that with only linear drawings, and particularly when ink is used.

You'll have greater control over the line quality if you can follow a single line for as long as possible without interruption. You should attempt this even if you know the line is not right. Always keep in mind that any line can be re-drawn, in the same fashion.

This is the best way for you to gain an understanding of the line in figure drawing. And you'll find that even if you make many lines in one area, they can still add to the overall quality of the drawing.

EXERCISE

Make several drawings in ink from poses of not more than 20 minutes. Be sure to include the whole figure. Try not to sketch with the pen. That is, take a line as far as possible without lifting the pen from the paper. Look carefully at the model and draw confidently, paying particular attention to the quality and expressiveness of the line.

Drawing With Pencil

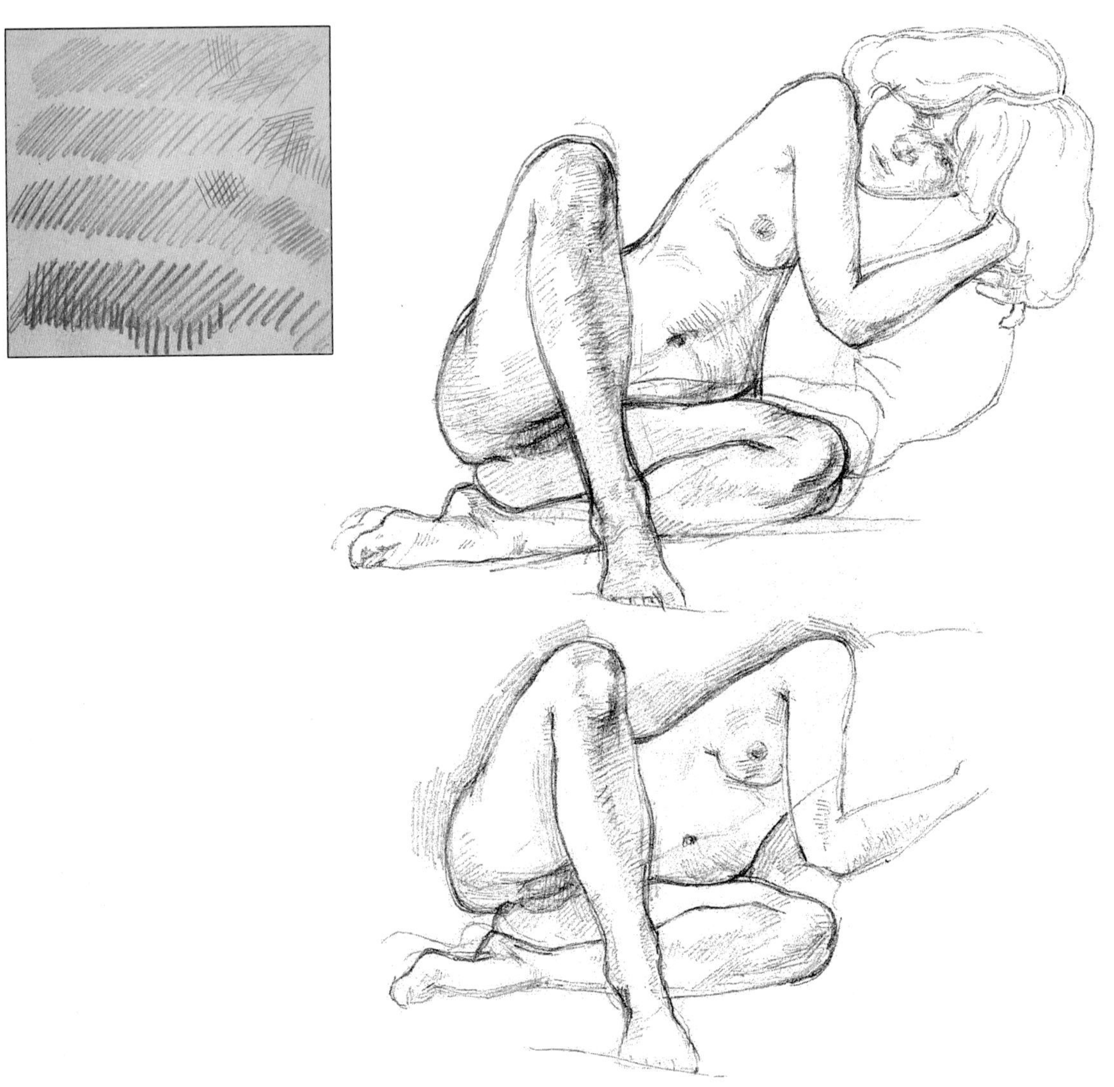

The next few sections cover different media you can use in making figure drawings. In addition, I'll discuss some techniques that correspond to each.

THE BASIC COMBINATION

The simplest and most standard method of drawing the figure is pencil on heavy, white writing paper. This combination is relatively straightforward, and will not demand the special considerations that some other media require.

I recommend that you work with a soft grade of pencil, because it will give you more flexibility than harder grades. With a soft pencil—such as a 2B—you can press lightly for a faint or sensitive line, and more firmly for a dark line or for shading.

Types of Pencil—The standard pencil is made largely of *graphite*. You can buy graphite drawing pencils in a range of grades.

In the center of the range is the HB pencil. The hardest pencil you can buy is 6H; the softest is 6B. For the purposes of figure drawing, pencils in the H range are seldom used. You will find the HB pencil and others of the B range most suitable.

Paper—No matter what medium you are using, paper is an important consideration. One factor to keep in mind is permanence: are you merely practicing, or are you making a drawing that you want to last? Apart from this, your choices regarding the color and texture of the paper are entirely personal.

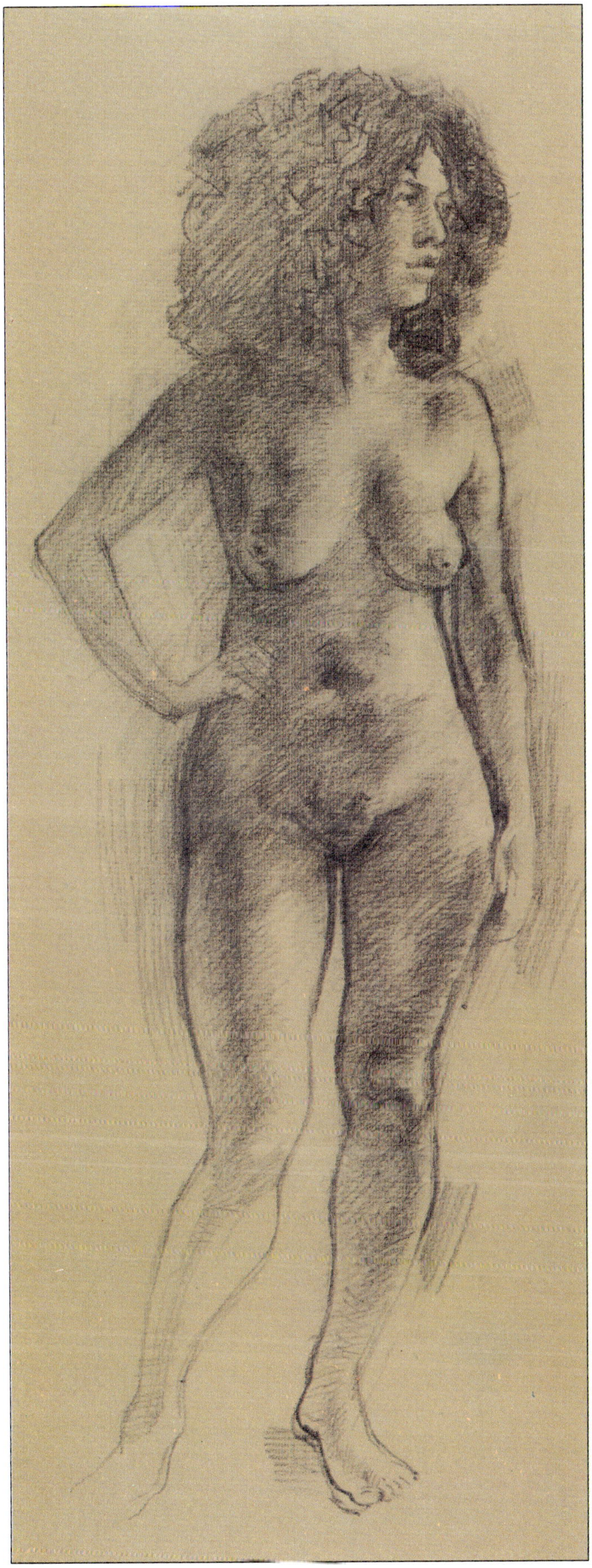

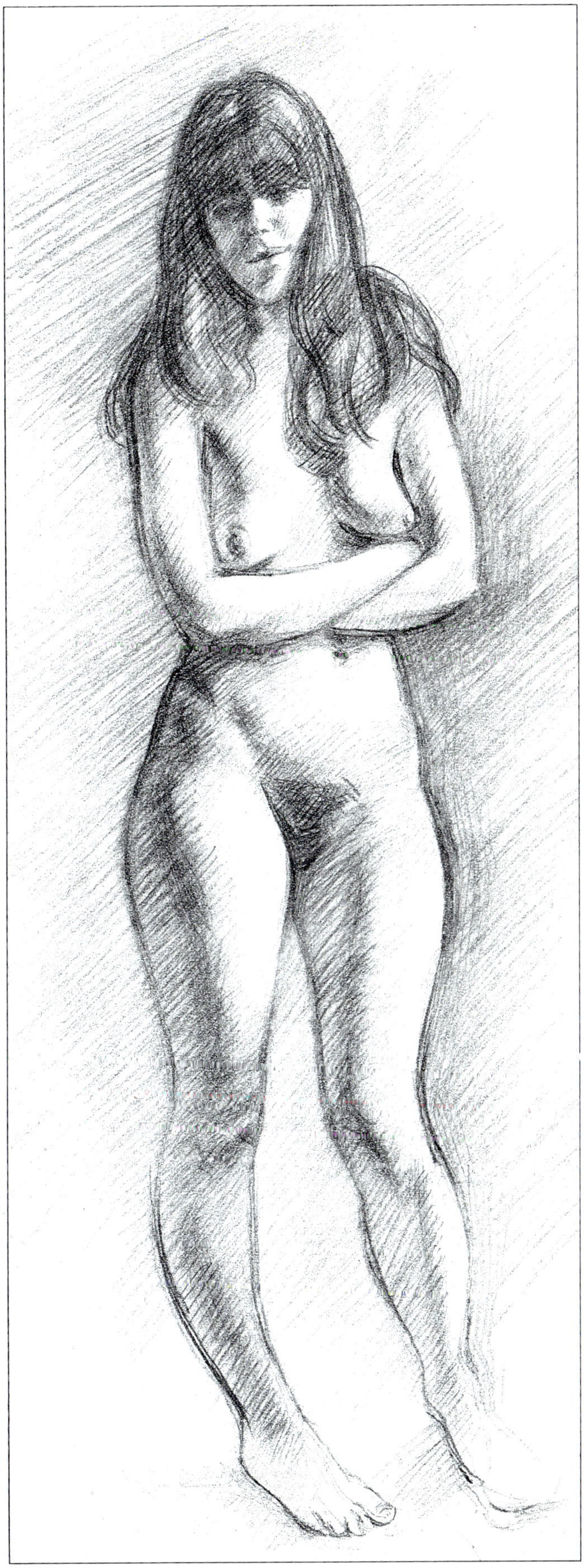

Drawing With Colored Pencils

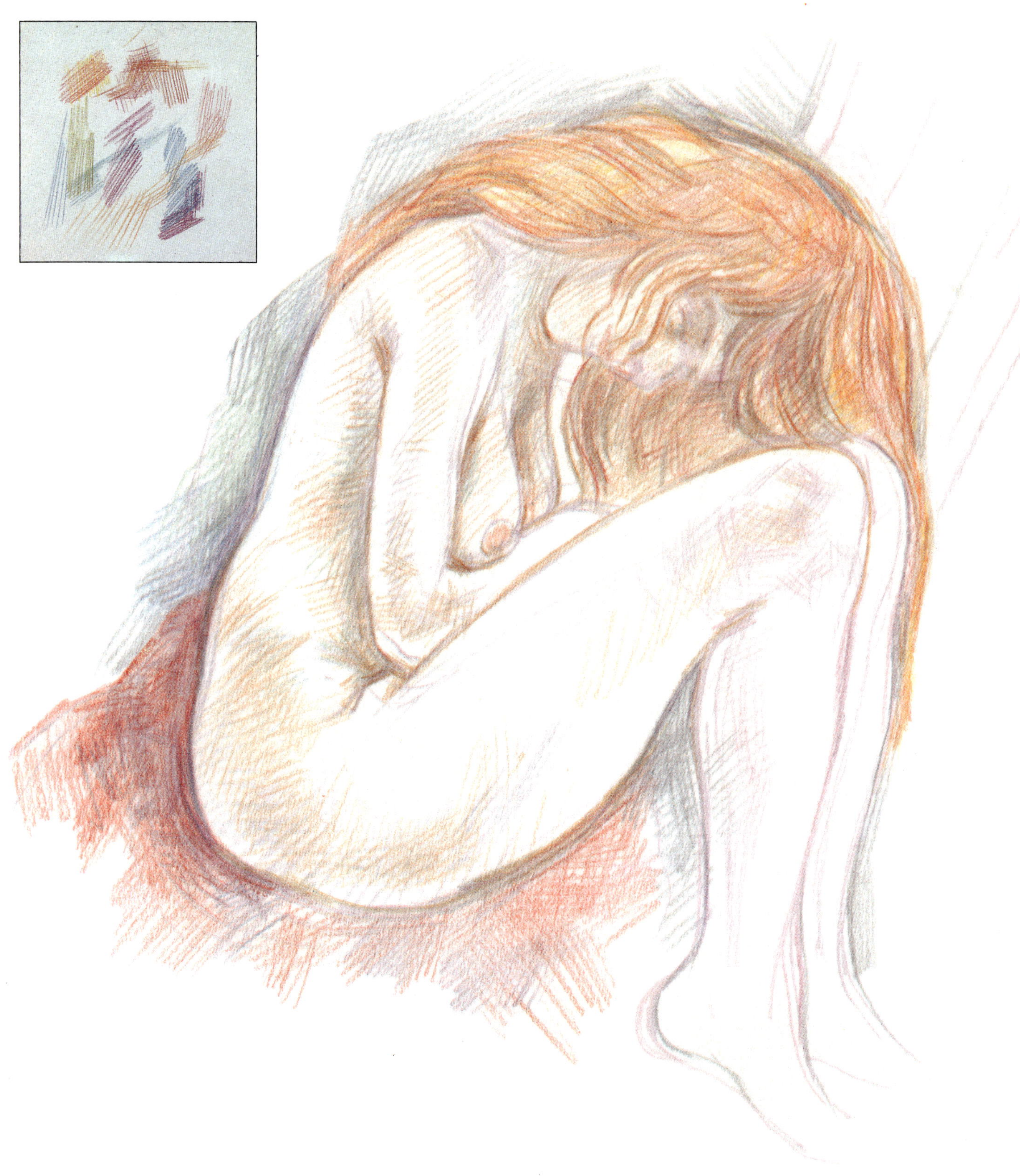

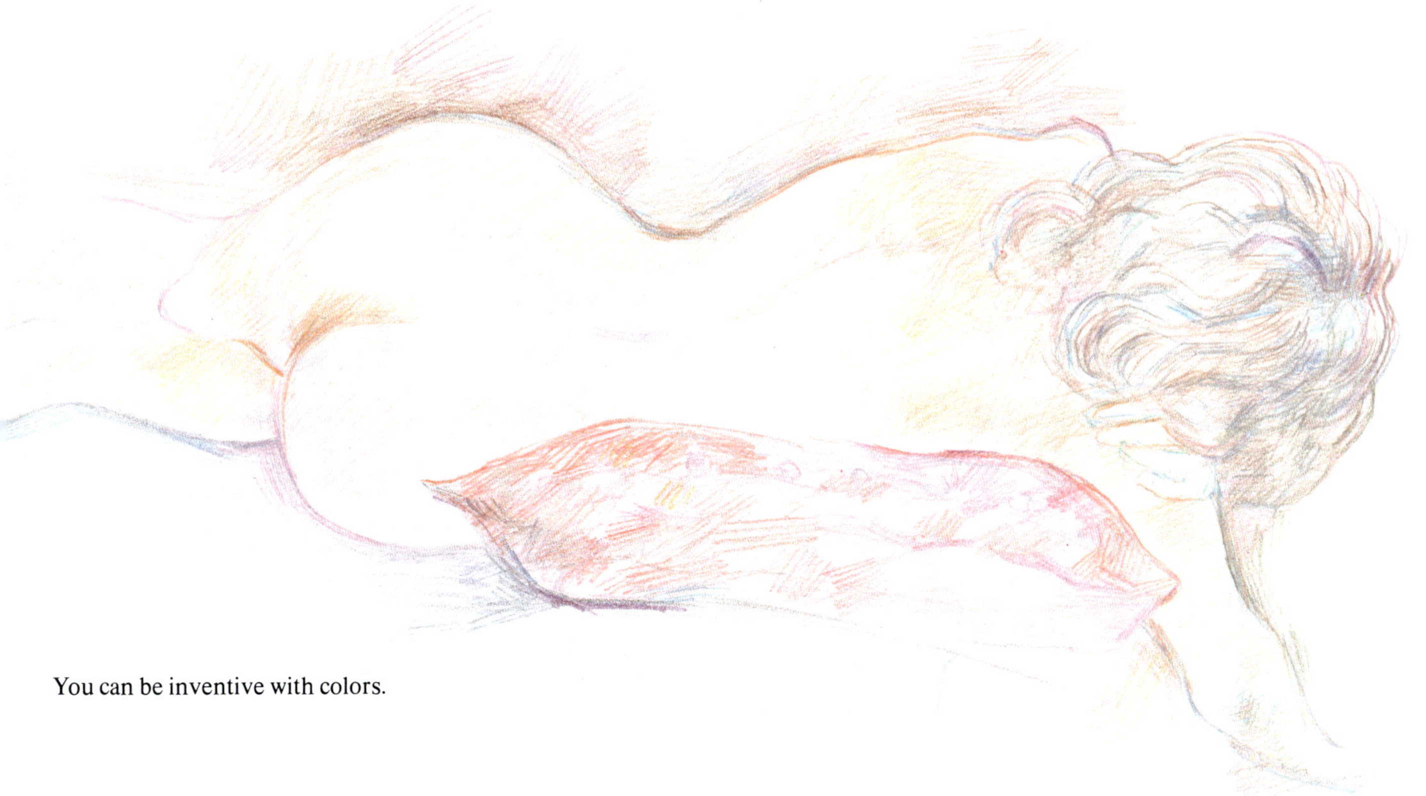

You can be inventive with colors.

Most of the media I discuss in this book—such as ink, oil paint and charcoal—have existed for centuries. But wax-based colored pencils are a fairly recent development. Wax pencils, or crayons, were first conceived of as a media for children. Now they are widely used in a refined form by artists and art students.

HOW TO USE COLORED PENCILS

You can use colored pencils on almost any type of paper. By gradually adding layer upon layer of color, you can achieve interesting effects. Although there is no "right" or "wrong" way to use these pencils, in my experience I have found it effective to build the image up gradually, using a *crosshatching* technique. You can see this technique in the drawings on these pages.

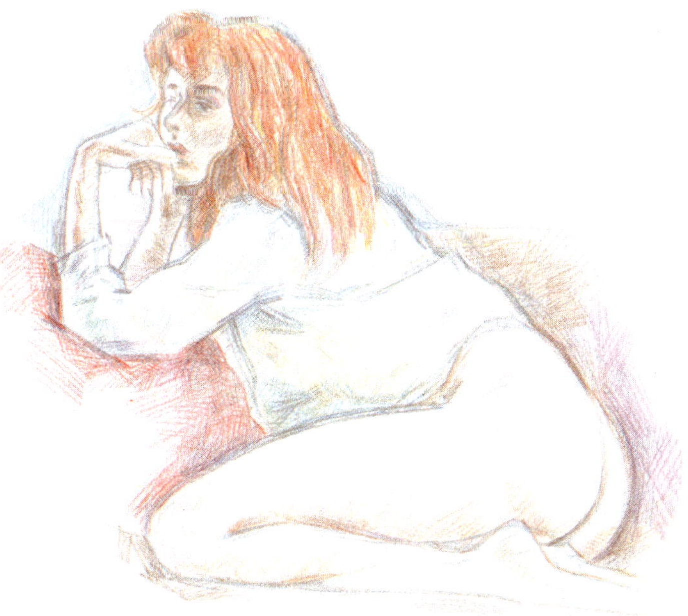

What to Buy—If you want an effect of full color, you will need to invest in a selection of a dozen or more pencils. This is because you cannot mix the colors in the way you mix colors of paint. Therefore, the wider your color selection, the easier it will be to achieve the effects you want.

Special Effects—Because of the color, these pencils give you possibilities that single-color media like the traditional pencil cannot. In the drawing on the previous page, the crimson cushion and the red-orange hair emphasize the pale, unbroken form of the model. This color contrast gives the drawing a quality it would not otherwise have. You should also notice that I minimized the color and the modeling on the surface of the figure, since my principle aim was to indicate overall shape.

Much the same is true of the drawing below. I intensified the color of the hair as well as the colors surrounding the figure. This heightens the effect of the pale, simple shape of the leg.

Be Creative with Color—The drawing above shows the delicate effect you can achieve with colored pencils. Notice also how I used the color in a somewhat inventive way. Rather than trying to imitate exactly the colors you see in a subject, you can use the pencils to enhance your attitudes about the model or pose. In other words, you can deliberately choose colors that may not exist in the subject, but seem to you to work well within the context of the drawing.

The drawings at right and on the opposite page show the gradual development of a drawing made with colored pencils. I deliberately changed the color from time to time—for no other reason than to keep the drawing "alive." If I needed to re-draw a part, the fresh color helped me to see the new lines more clearly.

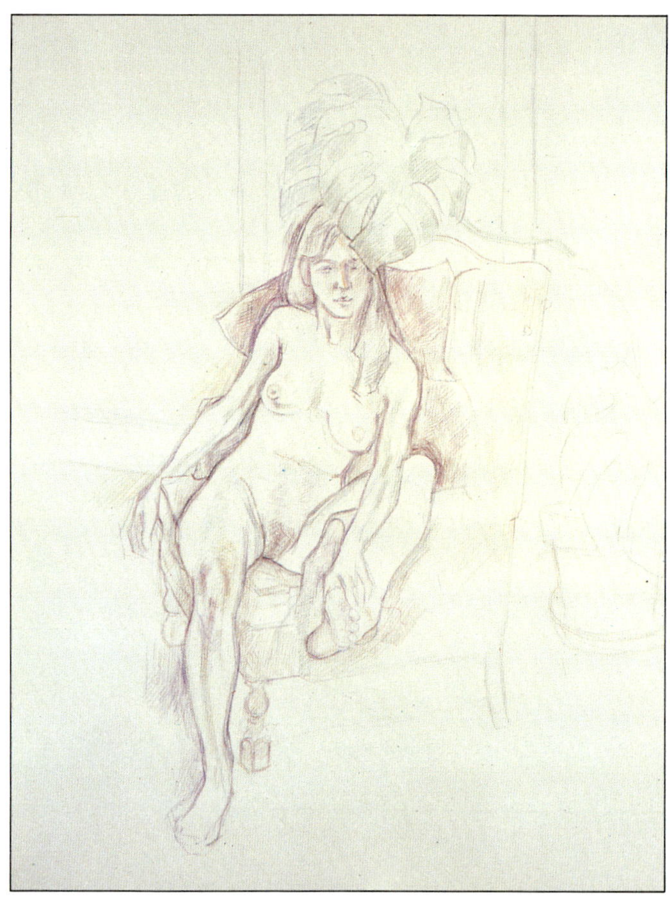

FIRST STAGE

To begin, I lightly sketched the basic form. In this initial stage there was no appreciable use of color around the figure.

Earlier I had become dissatisfied with the way the model's hair fell across her shoulders, and had asked her to push the hair back on one side. This proved effective for the drawing because it showed the junction of neck to shoulder more clearly, and also improved the design.

This is one of the few situations in which I would advocate erasing. Once I had decided that it was unsuitable to have the hair falling across the right shoulder, it became essential to erase that area. This is not the same as rubbing out every unsatisfactory line. In my opinion, such lines are a necessary part of the growth of a drawing.

SECOND STAGE

At this point I added more color to the objects surrounding the figure—chair, cushion and plant—and also to the figure itself. My purpose here was to further define the changes of plane and to add density to the whole drawing.

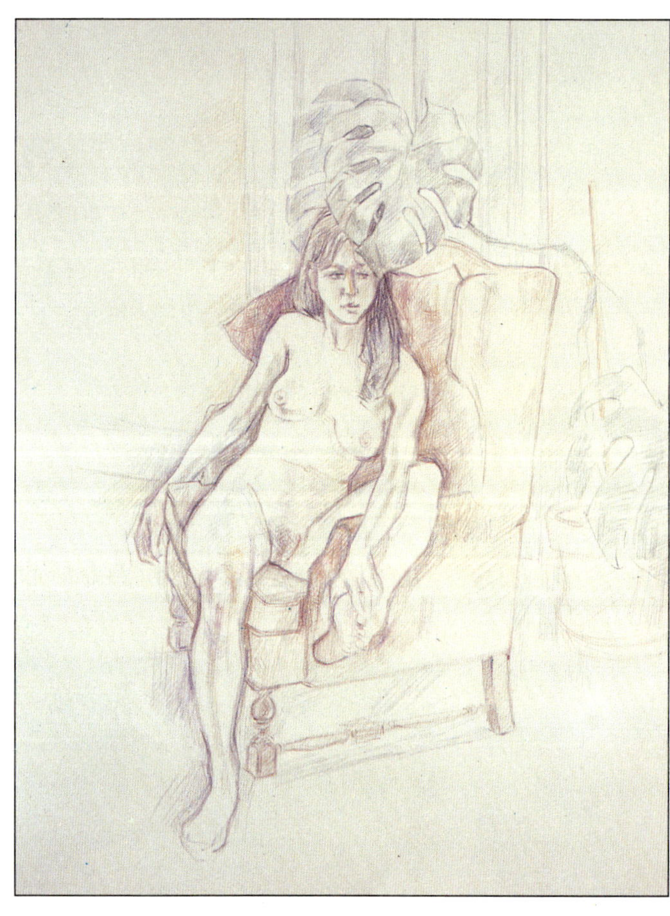

LAST STAGE

Between this stage and the previous one, I had second thoughts about the head, so I erased and redrew a part. You'll find that with a drawing of this sort, it becomes difficult to know when to stop. But by the time the drawing had reached this stage, I felt that the figure was quite well resolved, and the background was sufficient to make an interesting study.

Of course, there were parts that I could have continued to develop. But much of the charm of this medium lies in its sketchy, unfinished quality. In the case of this drawing, I thought at this point that it contained enough substance for me to stop working on it.

Above right: First stage.
Right: Second stage.
Opposite: Last stage.

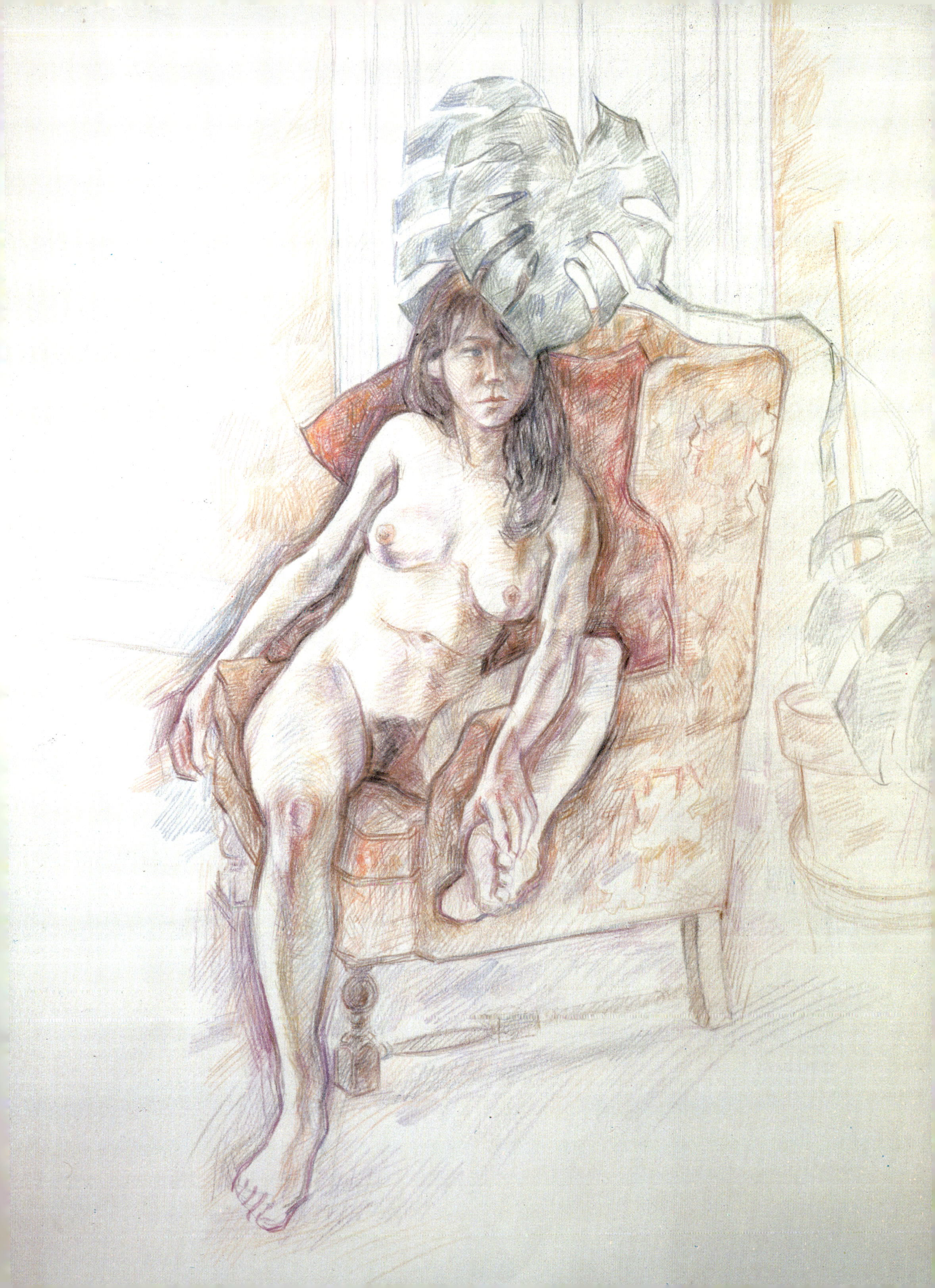

Drawing With Charcoal

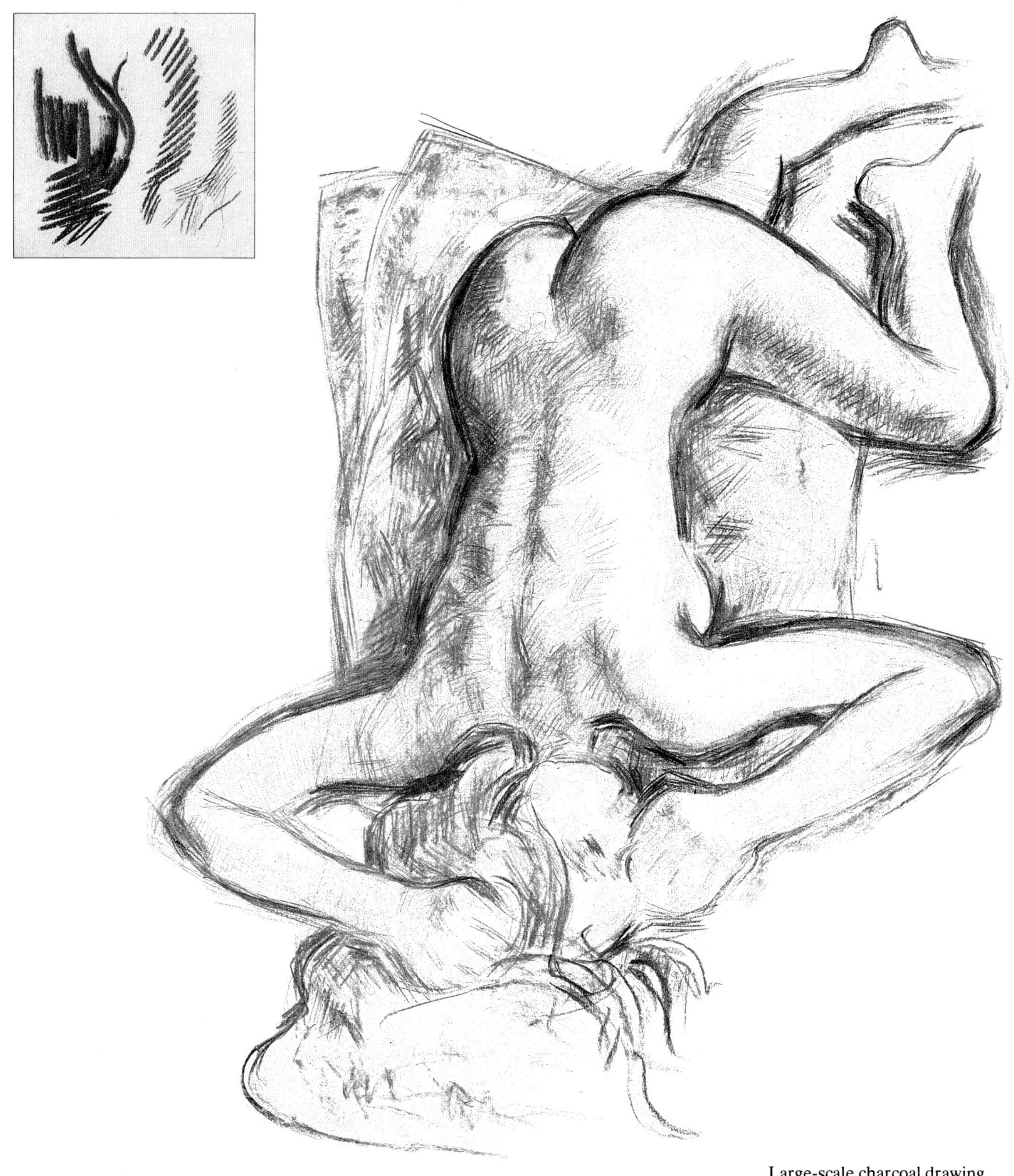

Large-scale charcoal drawing.

You might associate charcoal with large, black, and often messy drawings. It's true that charcoal is the ideal medium for expressive, forceful drawing. But it can also be excellent for smaller, more controlled work. I have always found charcoal to be one of the most sensitive and responsive media, and one you can use in most drawing situations.

CHARCOAL'S VERSATILITY

Charcoal usually comes in a box containing a number of sticks, each about six inches long. The sticks vary in thickness from about 1/2 inch to roughly the thickness of an ordinary pencil. You can even buy charcoal in the form of a pencil, which is quite convenient.

One advantage to using charcoal is that you can keep developing a drawing for a relatively long time without overworking it. This is because charcoal is very soft. In fact, it lies on the surface of the paper like a powder, making it easy to lift off with a putty eraser.

Charcoal also allows you to smudge and soften edges, moving from dark tones into light. One way to do this is to rub with a *stump.* It is simply paper bound tightly into the shape of a thick pencil. But many artists prefer to use their fingertips.

CHARCOAL IN LARGE AND SMALL DRAWINGS

The drawing on the previous page is 30 inches long and 20 inches wide. It was made with the thickest piece of charcoal available. Here I used my fingertips a great deal to soften the edges.

When you work on a scale this large, it's important to stand back regularly to observe the image. This is essential if you are to prevent serious errors in proportion. Because the image is so large when you are standing directly in front of the picture, you also need to stand back regularly to reduce the image size as you see it, and to observe the figure as a whole.

The drawings below were done with the smallest size of charcoal. Each of these originals is about one quarter the size of the original drawing on the opposite page. When you work on a small drawing in charcoal, practice supporting the drawing hand by pivoting it on the little finger. This keeps the palm off the drawing and helps you to avoid unwanted smudging.

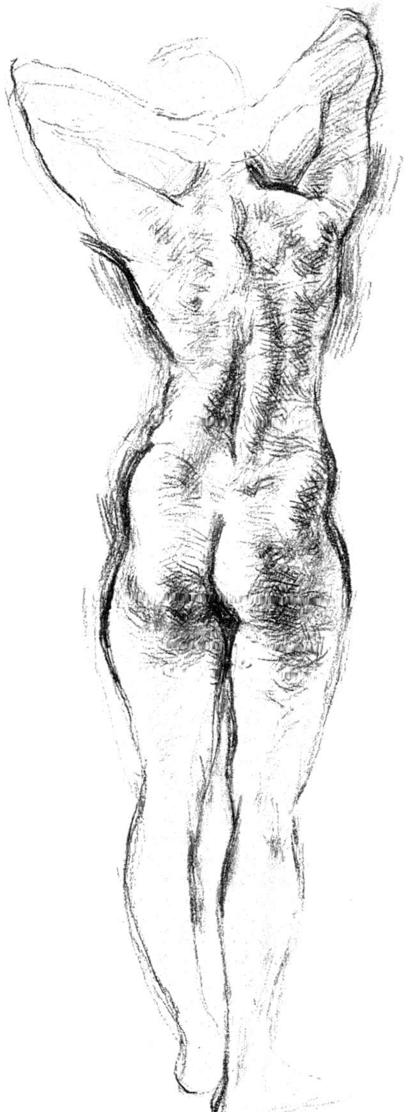

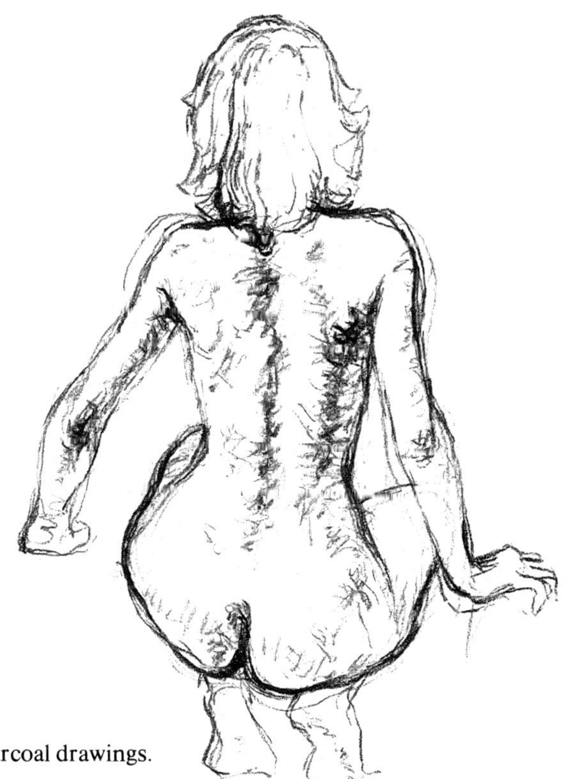

Smaller-scale charcoal drawings.

Drawing With Chalks

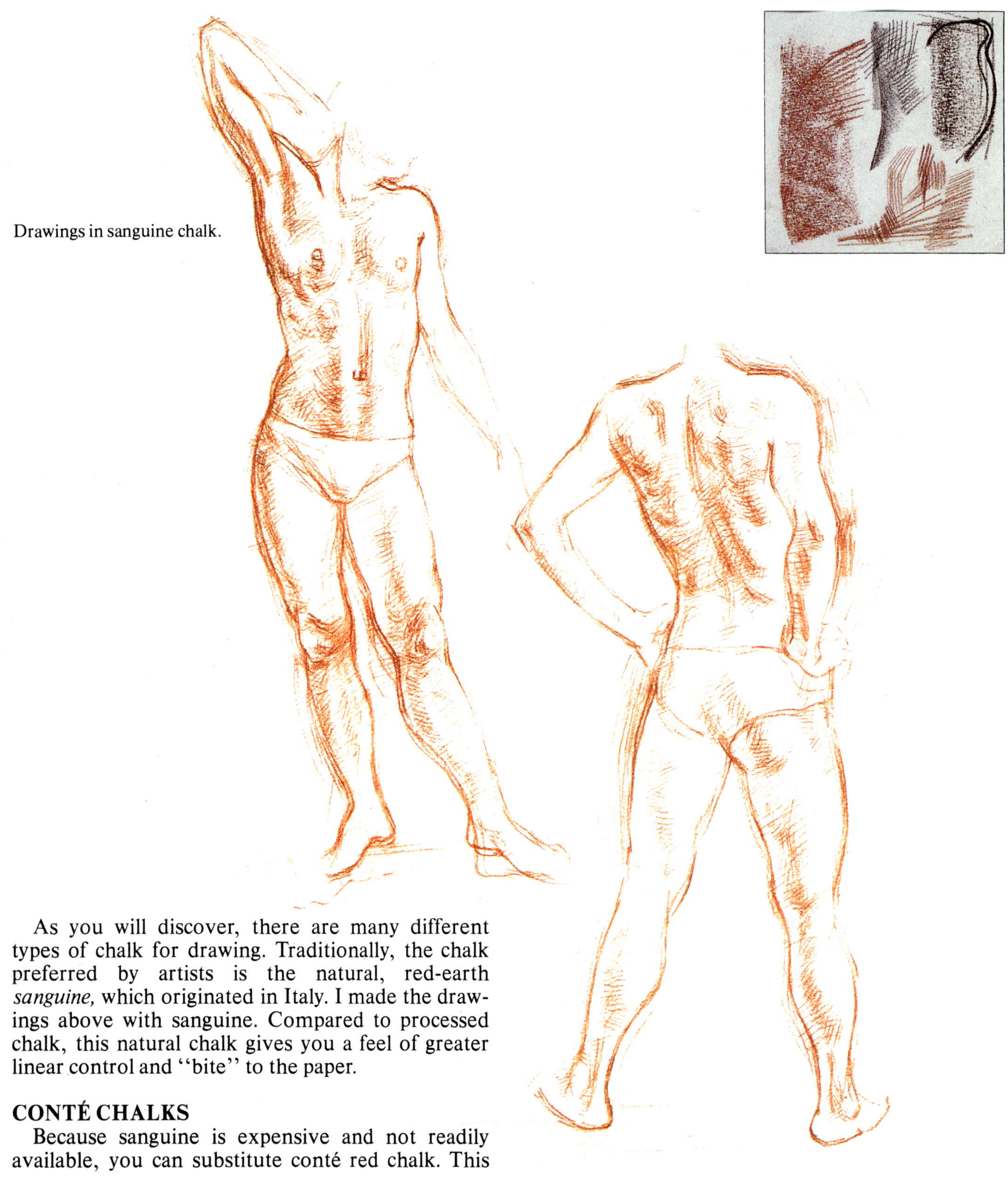

Drawings in sanguine chalk.

As you will discover, there are many different types of chalk for drawing. Traditionally, the chalk preferred by artists is the natural, red-earth *sanguine,* which originated in Italy. I made the drawings above with sanguine. Compared to processed chalk, this natural chalk gives you a feel of greater linear control and "bite" to the paper.

CONTÉ CHALKS

Because sanguine is expensive and not readily available, you can substitute conté red chalk. This

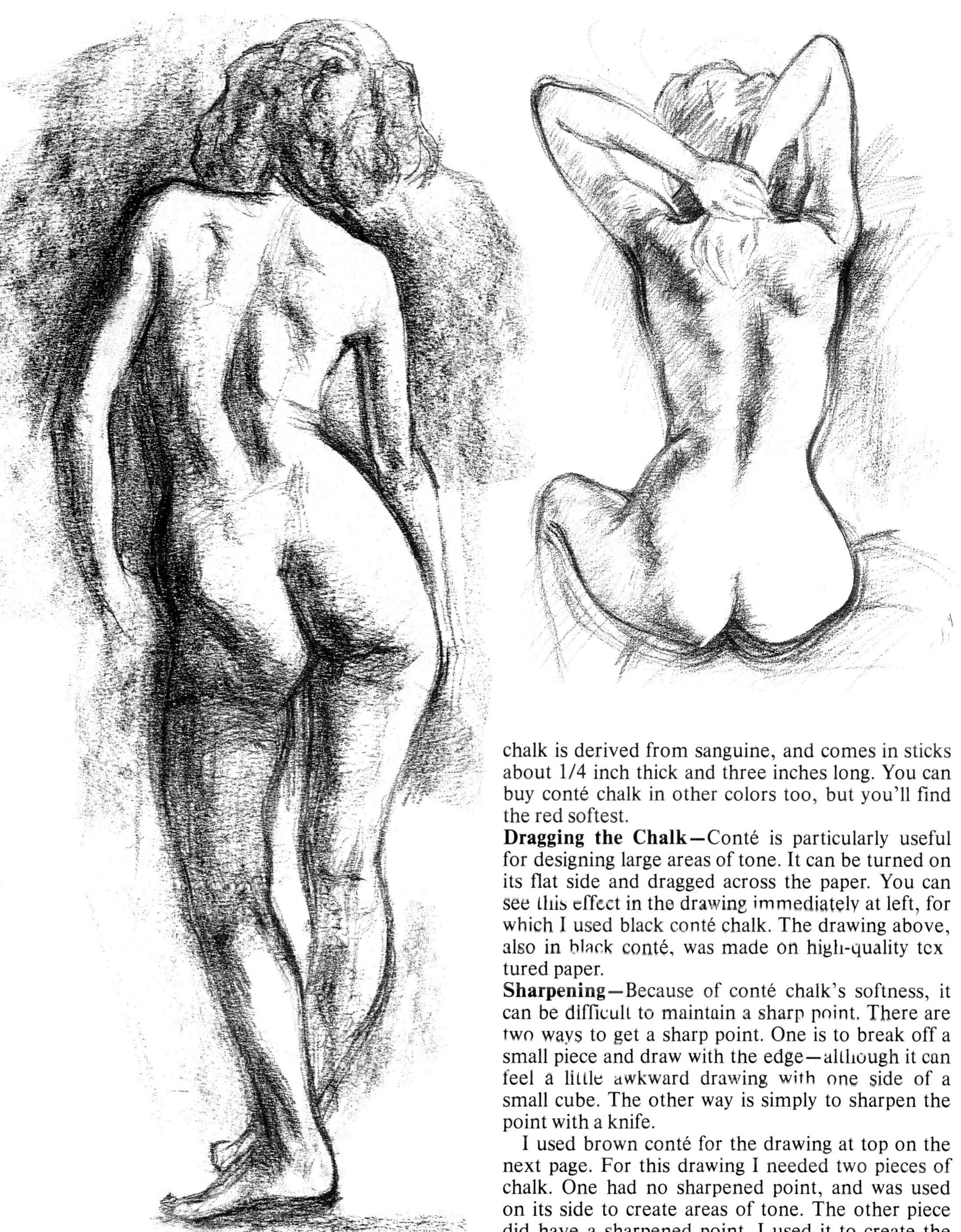

Drawings in black conté chalk.

chalk is derived from sanguine, and comes in sticks about 1/4 inch thick and three inches long. You can buy conté chalk in other colors too, but you'll find the red softest.

Dragging the Chalk—Conté is particularly useful for designing large areas of tone. It can be turned on its flat side and dragged across the paper. You can see this effect in the drawing immediately at left, for which I used black conté chalk. The drawing above, also in black conté, was made on high-quality textured paper.

Sharpening—Because of conté chalk's softness, it can be difficult to maintain a sharp point. There are two ways to get a sharp point. One is to break off a small piece and draw with the edge—although it can feel a little awkward drawing with one side of a small cube. The other way is simply to sharpen the point with a knife.

I used brown conté for the drawing at top on the next page. For this drawing I needed two pieces of chalk. One had no sharpened point, and was used on its side to create areas of tone. The other piece did have a sharpened point. I used it to create the linear form of the figure and to do further shading with lines.

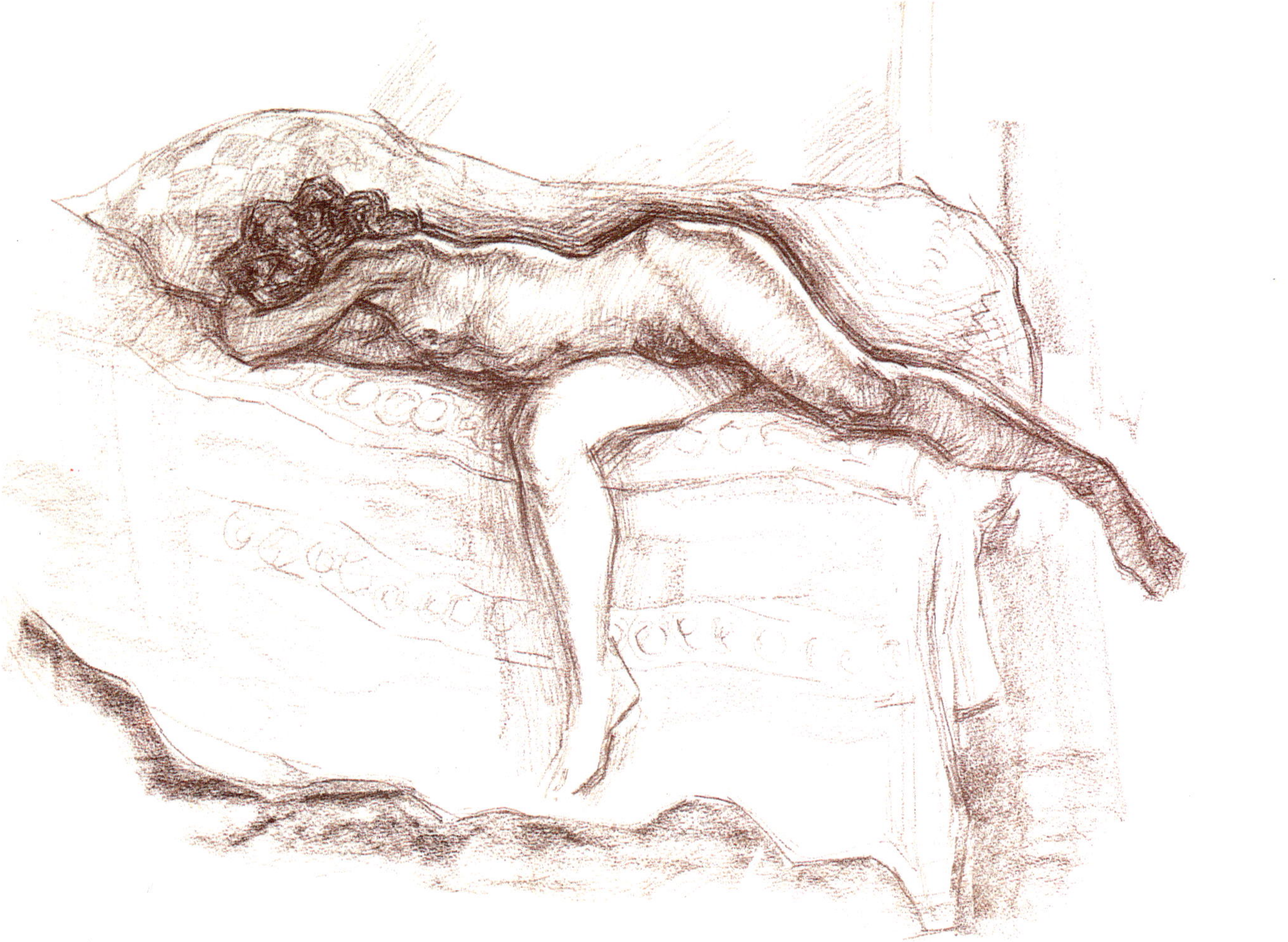

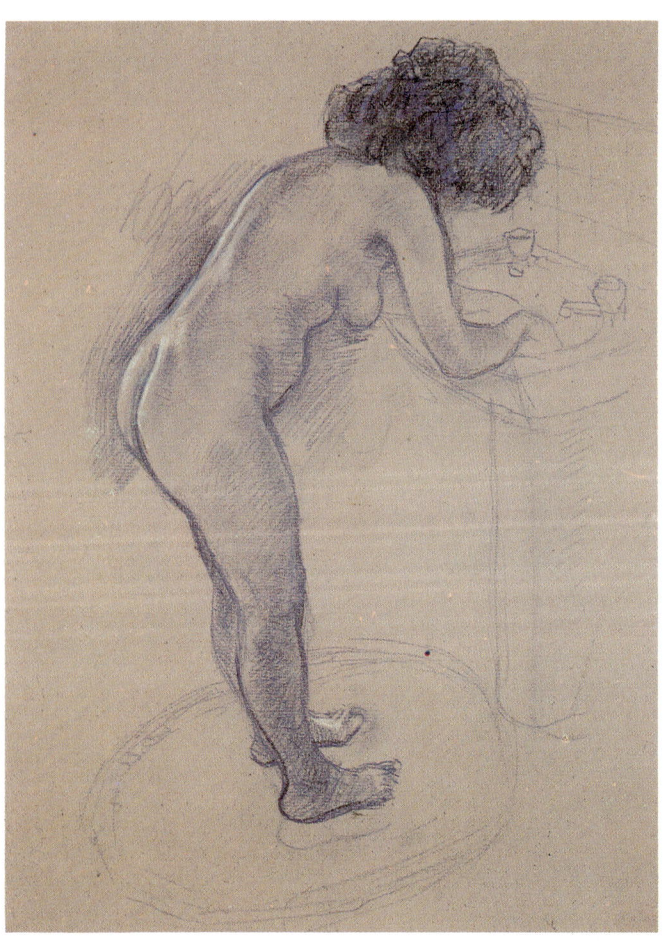

CHALK PENCILS

Like charcoal, chalk is available in pencil form. Charcoal pencil can be useful for making a detailed drawing requiring a consistent point.

Highlighting—The figure at left below was drawn in blue chalk pencil, which I heightened with white. When drawing on colored paper, you can use white chalk in this way as a subtle highlight. But this should be done sparingly.

Using a Sponge—The drawing at left on the opposite page shows one method of giving increased sensitivity to the chalk pencil. You do this by dampening the paper with a sponge, then drawing into the damp surface. Any mistakes can be wiped out immediately with the sponge.

I applied the same technique in the drawing at right on the opposite page, but in addition I used the sponge deliberately to make tones. If you plan to use a sponge in this way, be sure to begin with heavy-weight paper. Thinner papers, naturally, will begin to disintegrate after much rubbing with the sponge.

Above: Drawing in brown conté chalk.

Left: Drawing in blue chalk pencil.

Opposite: Drawings in chalk pencil on dampened surface.

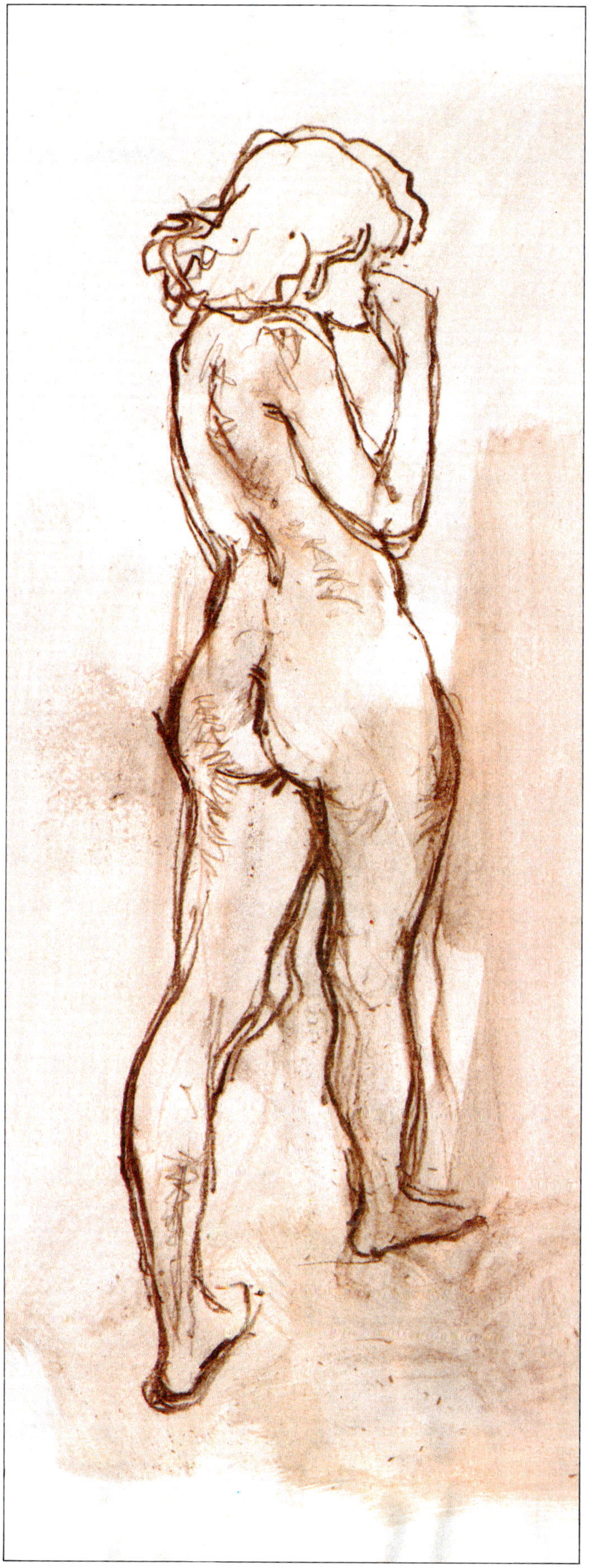

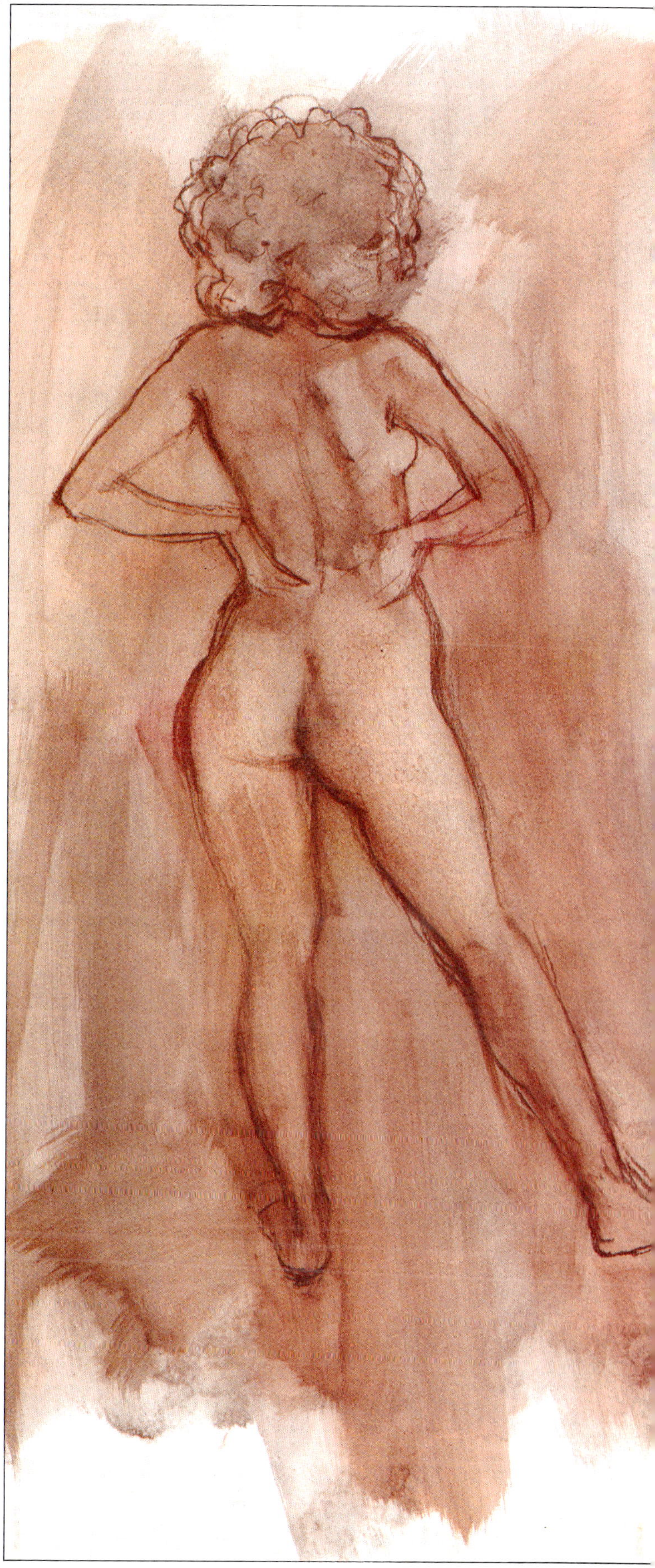

Drawing With Pastels

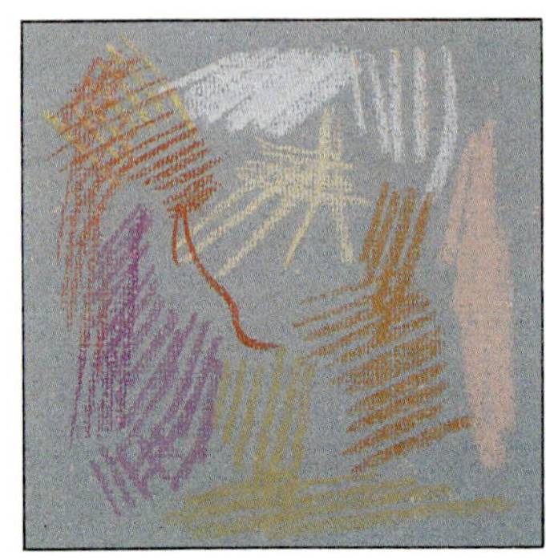

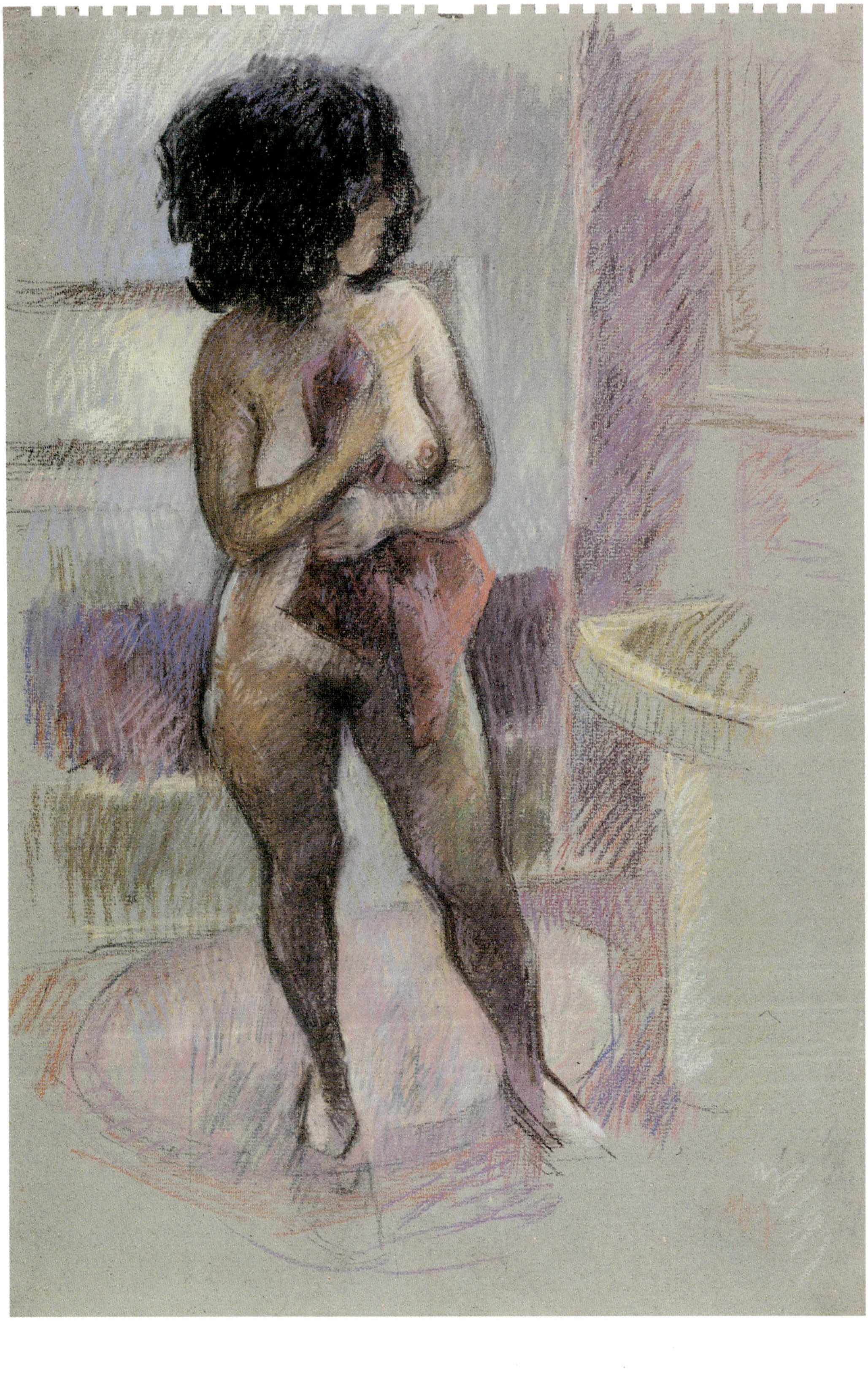

Pastels are similar to chalks. The composition of pastels is very simple—pigment with a small amount of binding medium. The advantages of pastels are that they have good covering power—giving your drawings an effect of fullness—and they are produced in a wide range of colors and tints. Because they are opaque, pastels are highly suited to working on toned paper.

PASTELS ARE UNIQUE

A finished pastel drawing, like those you see on these pages, resembles an oil painting in density. However, the approach and application differ greatly between the two media.

History—In the 18th century, artists made many highly-polished portraits in pastels, softening edges with a paper stump or smudging with a fingertip. These portraits were actually done in direct imitation of the traditional oil painting. However, since the innovations of French artist Edgar Degas (1834-1917), we tend to think of pastels as quite distinct from oil paints.

Building Color—When you use paints, you'll find that you rarely need more than a dozen different colors. This is because you can mix two, three or four colors together to achieve exactly the hue you desire.

But with pastels, the idea is to have a wide selection of ready-mixed tints. On the paper, you can blend pastels with your fingertip or with a cotton ball. After a certain point, however, the paper will become saturated and will not take any more pigment unless the paper is fixed.

There is another approach. Instead of blending the color on the paper, you can lay one color over another. By building up in this way, a little of each color shows through. This color-meshing technique is much closer to actual drawing than to painting, because you are adding individual lines stroke by stroke.

FIRST STAGE

Using a neutral gray sheet of Ingres rag paper, I began the drawing with a black pastel. At this stage I

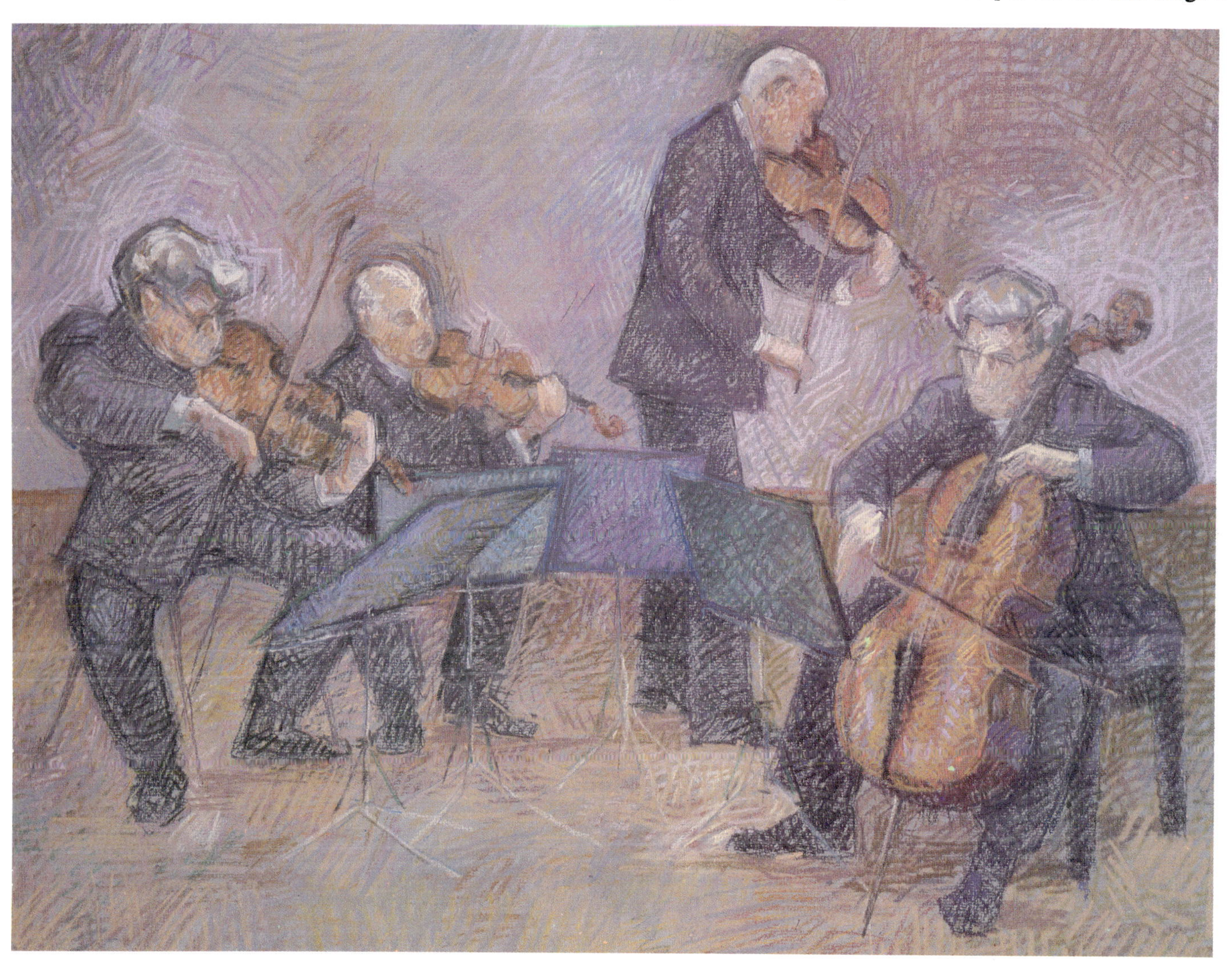

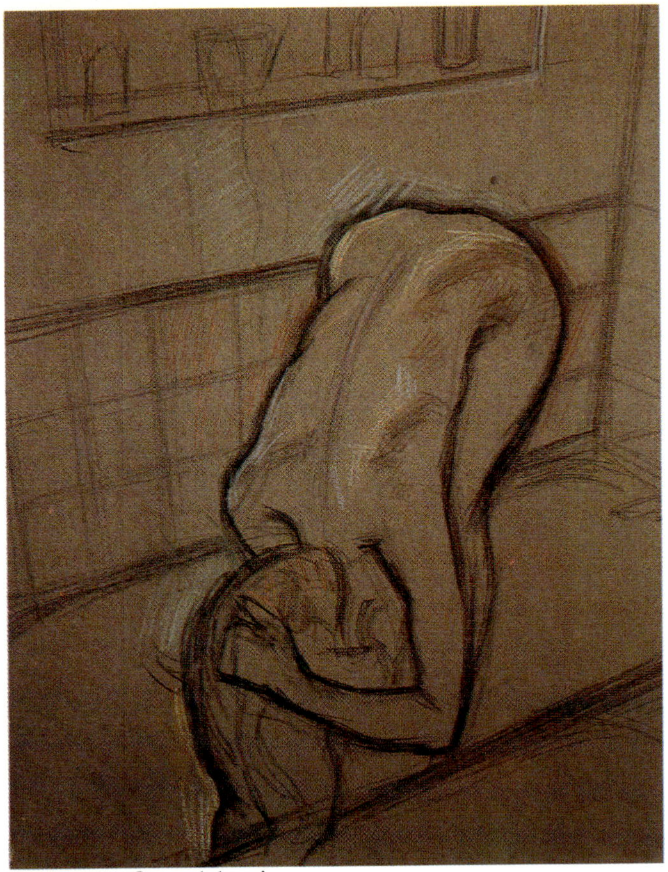

First stage of pastel drawing.

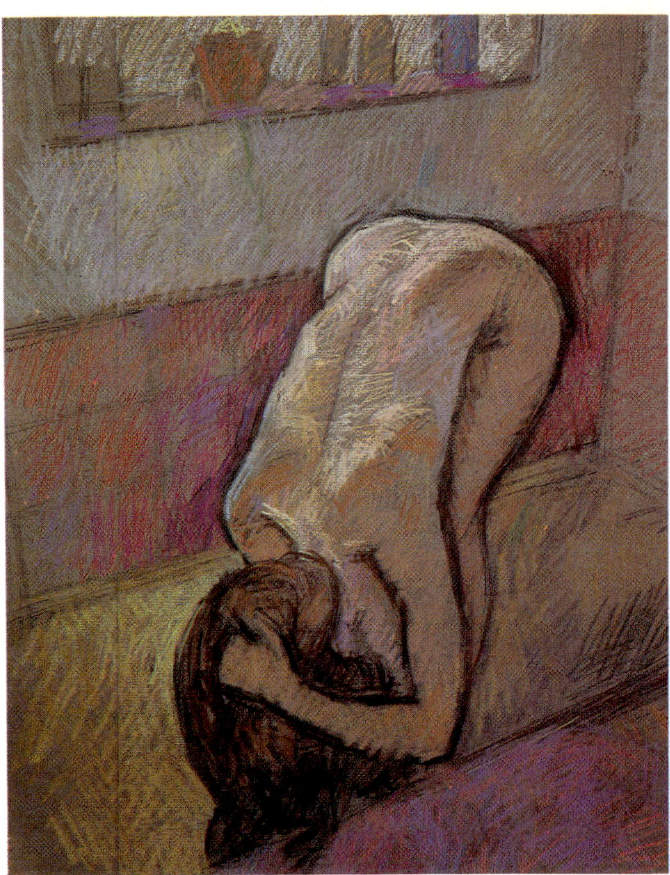

Second stage.

was particularly concerned with the composition of the drawing. I tried to block out a rough outline of the figure before continuing.

Once the figure seemed to be working on the page, I introduced some light colors, such as Lemon Yellow tint 0 and Yellow Ochre tint 0. My purpose here was to indicate certain high points on the back and to establish major changes of plane.

SECOND STAGE

Significant color was introduced at this stage. I tried to apply the color fairly evenly over the figure so that no single part received too much emphasis. Using a stroke-by-stroke technique, I applied suitable flesh tints such as Burnt Sienna, Red Gray, Burnt Umber and Reddish Purple. I was aware that at this point some of the colors, especially on the figure itself, were too bright. But I knew these areas would be worked over, so that eventually only patches of the bright color would show through.

LAST STAGE

Apart from a few background changes, such as the addition of a pot on the window ledge, I now concentrated on completing the development of the figure. Notice that the contours have now been lost because the edges are defined with colors. Some of the bright orange and mauve colors on the back were modified and worked into the overall form.

In the entire process of making this pastel drawing, I did not rub out any mark. If I thought that a part needed adjusting, I made the changes by adding a layer of color over the top, or by placing a color next to the unsatisfactory area to alter its relative effect.

Fixing the Pastel—By the time I stopped working on this pastel, the paper surface was almost saturated and was ready for fixing. When you reach this saturation stage with a pastel, it is generally advisable to spray it with chemical fixative. This is especially important if you want to continue working on the drawing. There is a limit to how much the paper surface will hold before the pigment begins to fall off as powder. If a pastel is framed under glass as soon as it is complete, then fixing is not usually as necessary.

Opposite: Last stage.

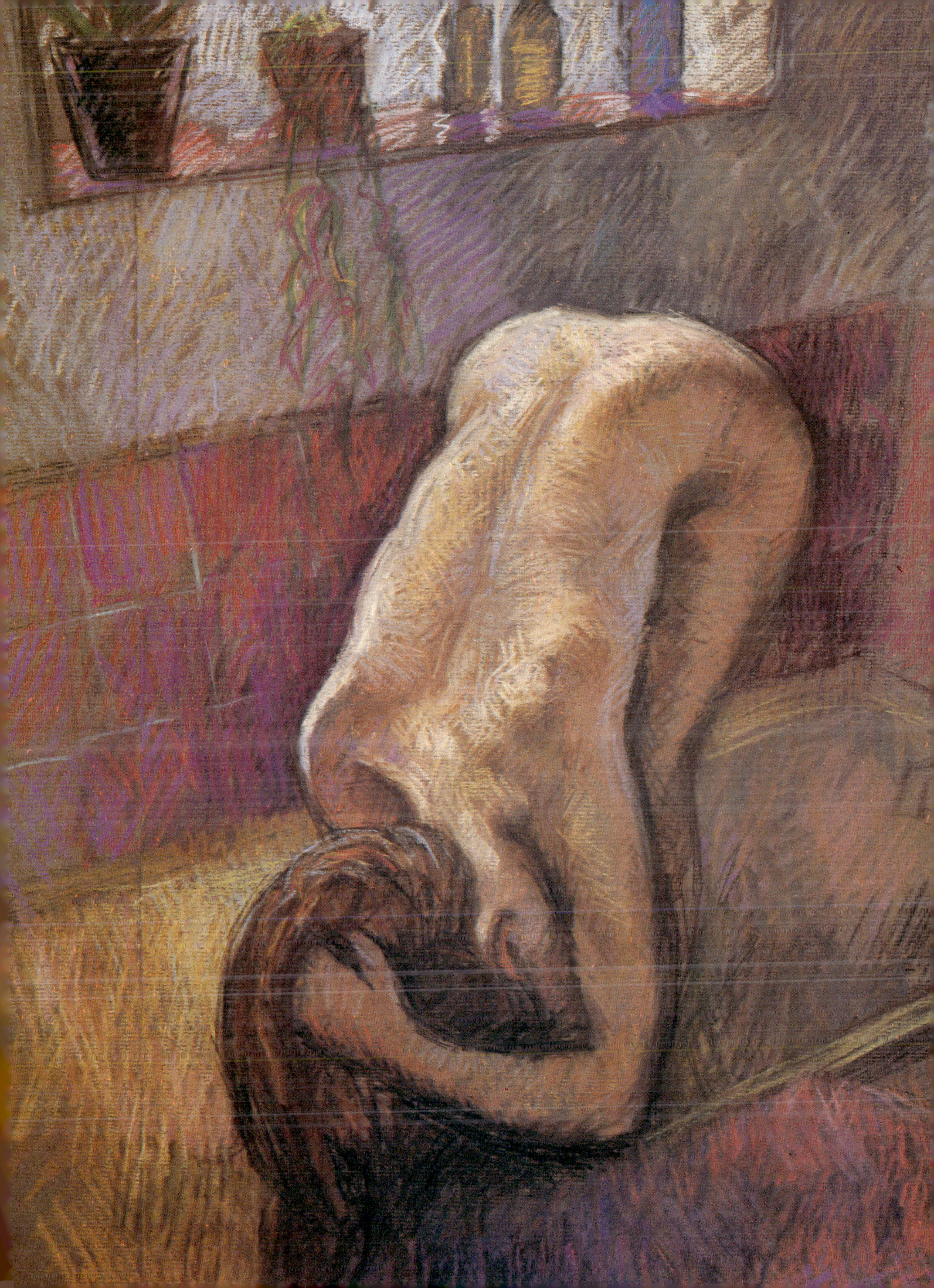

Drawing With Ink

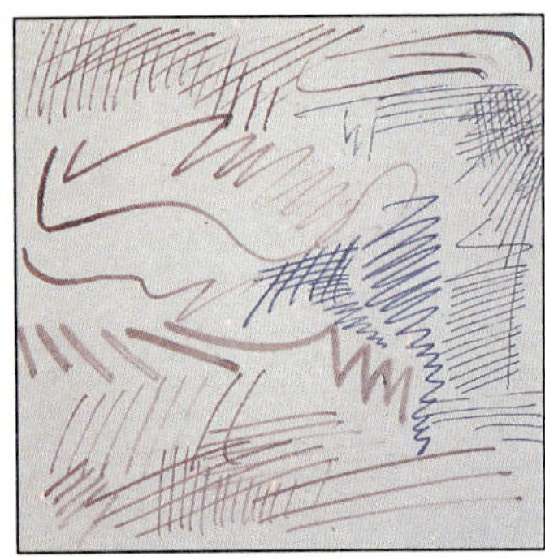

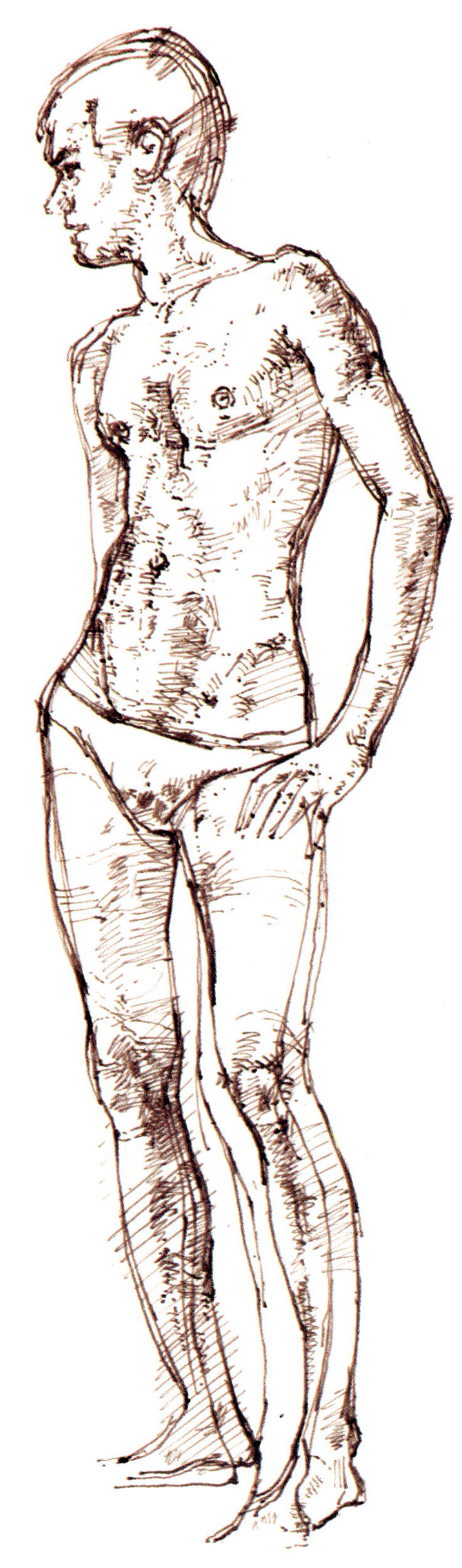

If you're a beginner, the idea of making a figure drawing in ink can be a little frightening. Why? Because ink cannot be erased. Some people are so worried about making indelible mistakes that they avoid ink completely. But as far as I am concerned, when drawing from life there is no such thing as a mistake.

SOME CONSIDERATIONS

If you think of a drawing as a series of approximations, then every mark helps gauge the next. A drawing is built up by an accumulation of marks, each defining the shape a little more. You'll discover that as your drawing progresses, each mark becomes less of an approximation and more of a positive intention. If you adopt this approach, you'll see each stage of a drawing—including the original exploratory statements—as a valuable part of the whole.

With this in mind, you can begin a drawing in ink without any fear of the results. In fact, I believe that practicing in ink can strengthen your all-around ability to draw the human figure. I have concluded that drawing in ink helps students in two basic ways. First, students tend to overcome their initial fear of first statements. And second, they learn to observe more accurately, and therefore achieve a greater economy of lines.

Length of Poses—With ink, as with any other medium, the degree of finish or content will depend in part on the length of the pose. Short poses of 10 to 15 minutes are usually ideal for pen drawing, to explore the purely linear qualities of a figure. But you may also want to spend three or four hours on a pose, working to achieve density and fullness. The ink drawing on page 14 is an example of a finely worked figure resulting from a longer pose.

TYPES OF PENS

What sort of pen should you use? The most common type for figure drawing is a *dip pen* with a bottle of ink. But there are many other types of pens available for you to experiment with. You can see a few of these pens in the photograph on page 6.

The *steel-nib pen* with reservoir is another common type. The *reed pen,* as its name suggests, is made from a reed. It is inexpensive and has a beautiful touch. The *quill pen* is made from a goose feather, giving it a very different feel from the previous two pens.

A *fountain pen* is inexpensive and convenient. But do not try to use it with India ink or any waterproof ink—the shellac in the ink will clog the pen. Rapidograph-type *technical pens* have a hard, inflexible nib that provides consistency in the thickness of the line. Finally, *felt-tip pens* can be useful for drawing, but because their ink is impermanent, you should use them only for sketchbook drawings.

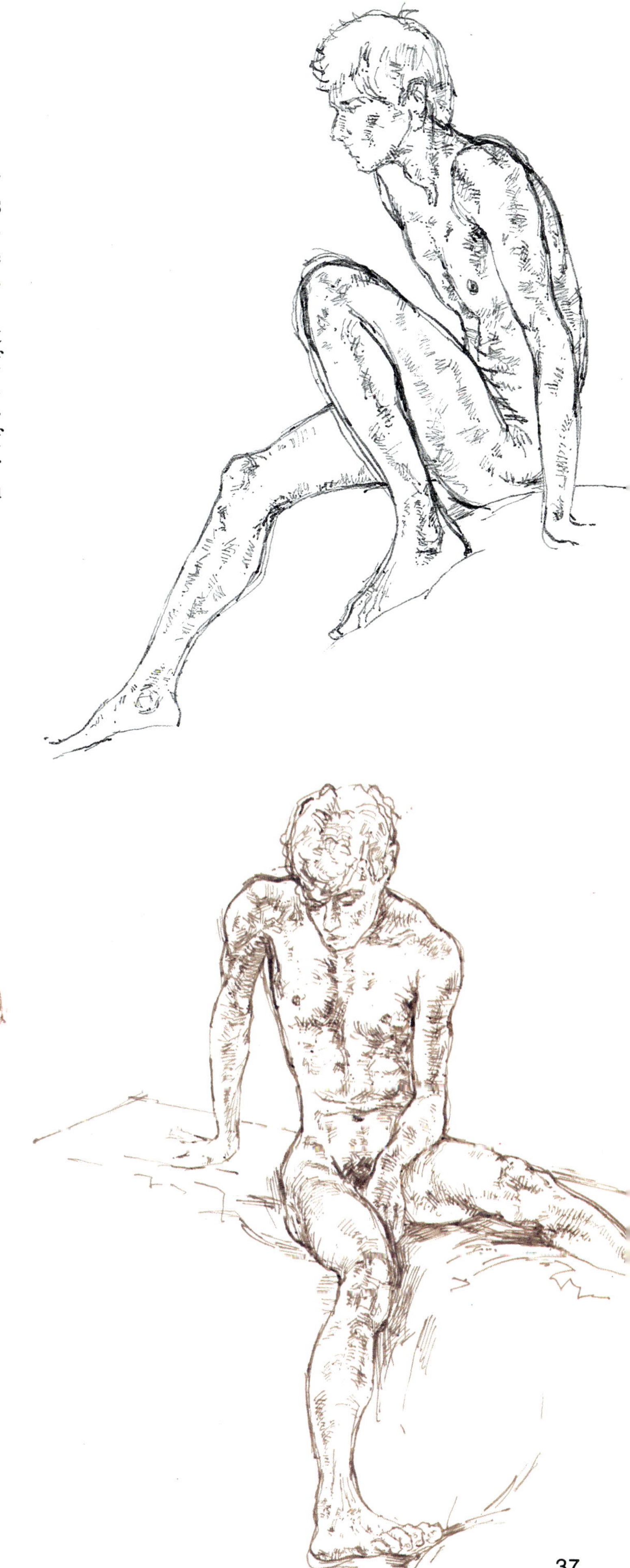

Using Pencil And Wash

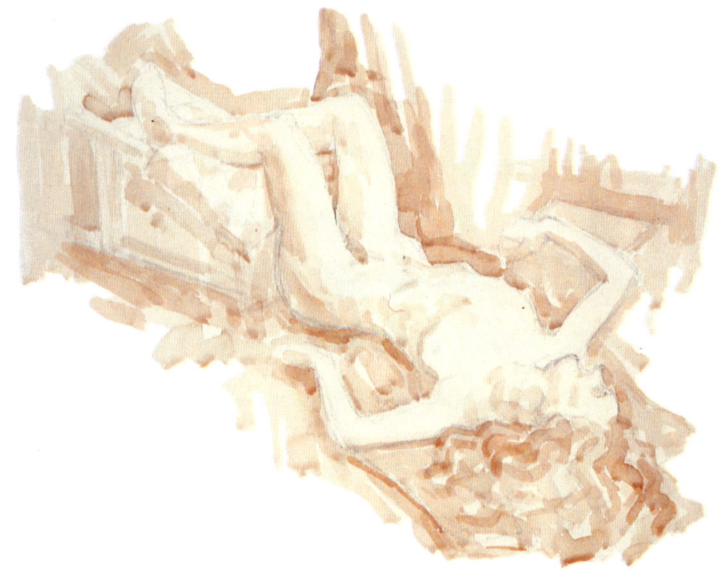

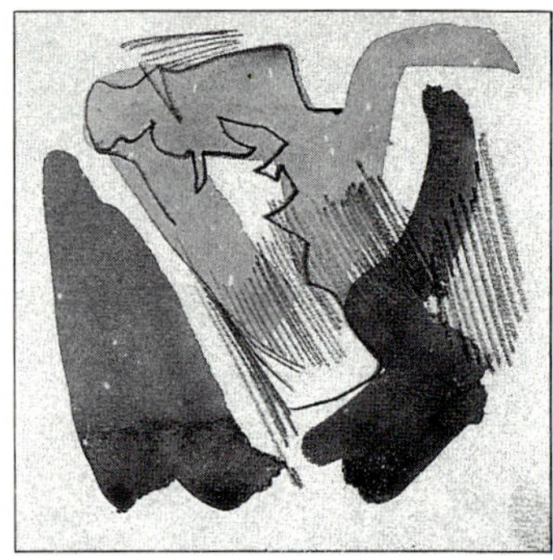

First stage.

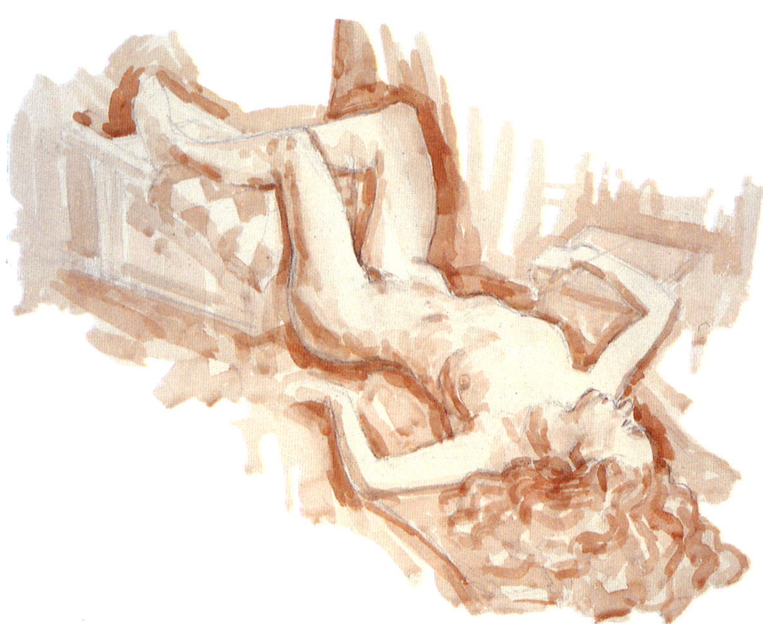

Second stage.

A *wash* can be either diluted ink or ordinary watercolor paint. You will need one medium-sized, good-quality brush. If the brush comes to a fairly sharp point, it will lay a wide wash in addition to giving relatively delicate lines.

TIPS FOR USING WASH

You may want to try using a pen or a pencil along with the wash for "sharpening up" parts of the drawing. I prefer pencil because of its neutral color and because, like chalk, its effect can be improved if used on damp paper.

When making wash drawings, I find it useful to pre-mix three stages of wash: pale, medium and dark. I lay the first wash over every area that does not "receive light" directly. Then I add the second and finally the third mix to further darken and define certain areas.

FIRST STAGE

I began the drawing of the reclining nude by broadly indicating in pencil the basic elements of the composition, such as the figure, the cushion and the supports. When I was satisfied with the arrangement, I introduced a pale wash to define the main tonal areas.

SECOND STAGE

After the initial wash, I introduced a darker mix to continue strengthening the drawing. This was done not only by working on the figure itself, but also by establishing surrounding tones. The right leg, the forehead and the torso are gaining more shape.

LAST STAGE

In this stage, the whole image darkens, and the character of the pose becomes more complete. I added to and darkened the background to create greater contrast with the light areas on the figure. Changes of plane on the torso are also more defined.

About halfway through the drawing, I used the pencil to define certain areas more sharply—such as the head, right arm and left leg. But it is still the wash that gives this drawing its basic character, with broadly defined areas of shape and tone not so easily achieved with pencils or other media.

EXERCISE

Pose your model in strong, consistent light for three hours, taking breaks when necessary. Pre-mix three stages of wash in separate pans, using ink or any single shade of watercolor. Begin with a very brief pencil sketch to roughly define the shape of the figure and background objects. Introduce the wash as soon as possible. Continue developing the drawing through the final wash, strengthening with a pencil those parts of the drawing you think lack definition.

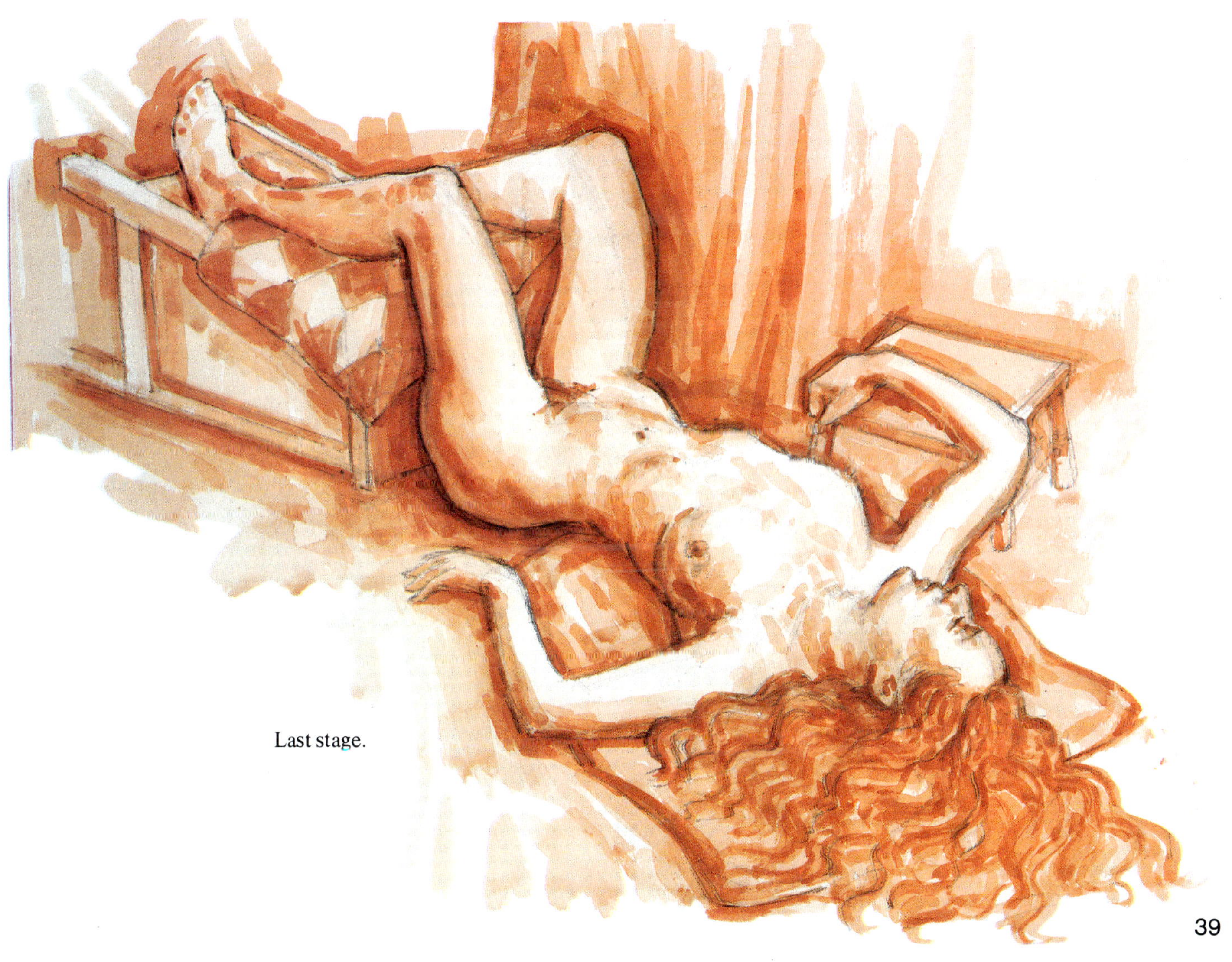

Last stage.

Using Watercolor

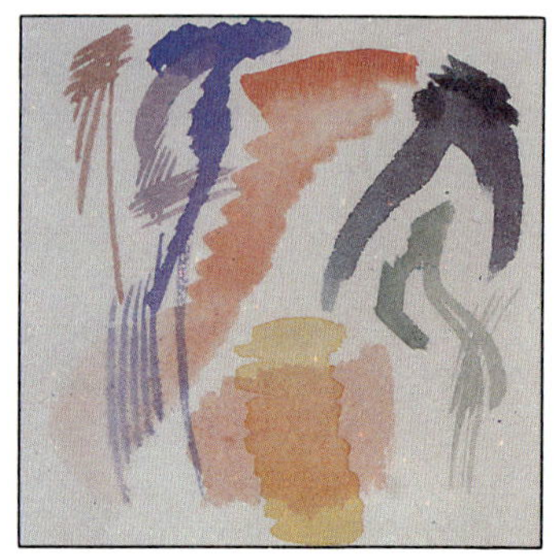

Watercolor paintings are often mistakenly called *watercolor drawings.* In fact, all watercolors have traditionally been referred to as *drawings,* probably because paintings using this medium in a single color were common in the 18th and 19th centuries.

DRAWING FROM LIFE WITH WATERCOLOR

Watercolor is an excellent medium to use for figure drawing. Although it seems to lend itself to painting, especially to landscape painting, this medium offers both versatility and convenience for figure work.

Adding Pencil—I often use pencil along with watercolor to "sharpen" parts of a drawing at later stages—much the same as with an ink wash. However, to get the greatest value and joy out of this medium, you'll want to use the brush alone in early stages of the drawing.

Fig. 11) Left: Watercolor drawing from 15-minute pose.

Fig. 12) Below: This watercolor drawing has marks to indicate structure rather than tone.

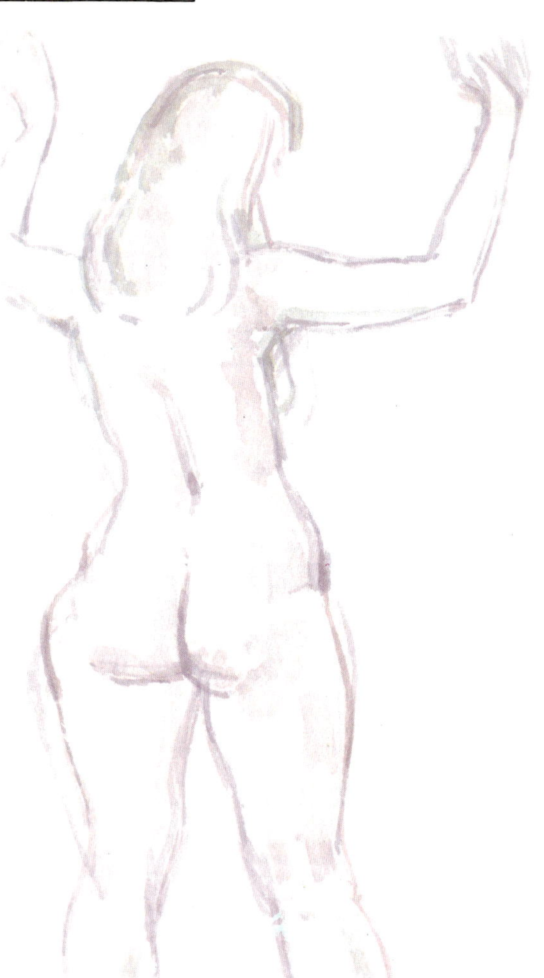

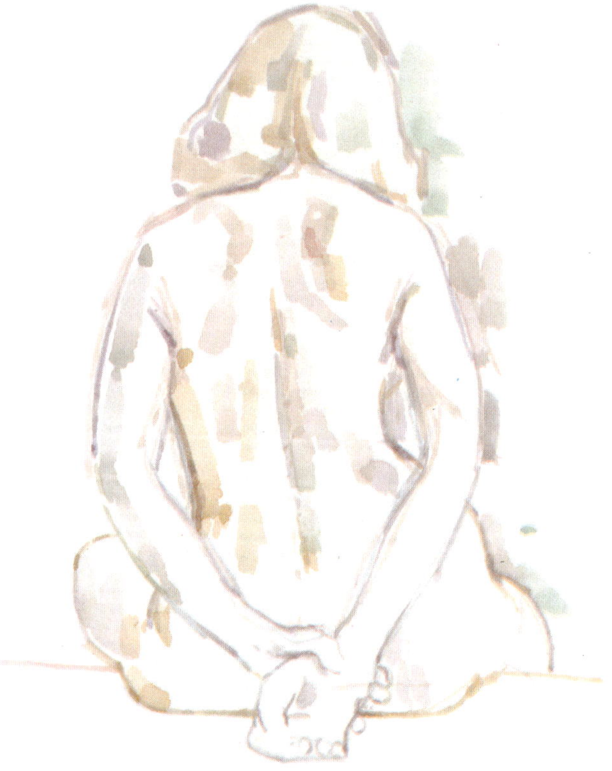

The Brush—A watercolor brush is suitable for stating large shadow areas quickly and effectively, as well as for depicting lines. You can achieve both of these effects with a single, good-quality brush that comes to a sharp point. I recommend that you invest in a sable brush. Though expensive, this brush will serve you well for a long time if you care for it properly.

You will be able to sense a great difference between the feel of a brush and the feel of pencils or pastels. Working with a brush forces you to simplify—and probably to think harder before making a line. With pencils and pastels, it's easy to slip into a tentative and sketchy method. A session with the brush can produce some boldly stated, but sensitive, drawings.

Short Poses—I find that watercolor works best for relatively short poses. I drew the figures on the previous page from 15-minute poses, with just a brush and some dilute color. Both figures show an attempt to indicate structure alone, with no real tonal areas.

Color—The color you use in watercolor drawings does not really matter. In fact, it's a good idea to vary the color as you correct or slightly alter lines. You can change the color to indicate changes in the figure's structure, or even for decorative effect.

Boxes—You can buy watercolor boxes in various sizes, ranging from a small pocket size to a large studio box. Both these types are illustrated in the photograph on page 7. It's possible to manage without a box at all, by purchasing individual pans of color and mixing them on a separate palette. But I recommend a box because it holds all of the colors in one place and has a built-in mixing tray.

DIFFERENT WATERCOLOR EFFECTS

I drew the seated nude in figure 13 as a demonstration for students. For this I used a large, studio-watercolor box with an additional mixing pan. The mixing pan was necessary because I used large areas

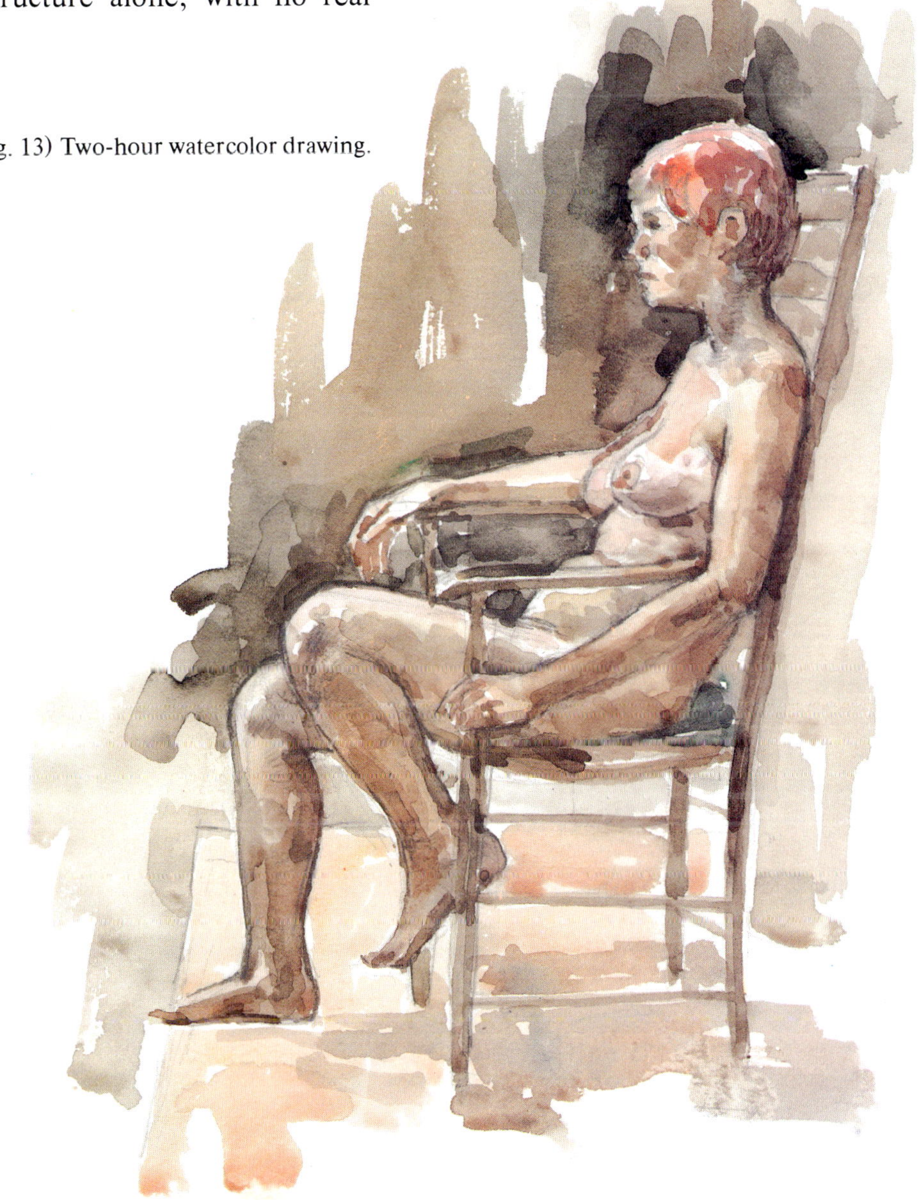

Fig. 13) Two-hour watercolor drawing.

Fig. 14) 20-minute watercolor drawing. Here I used no pencil at all.

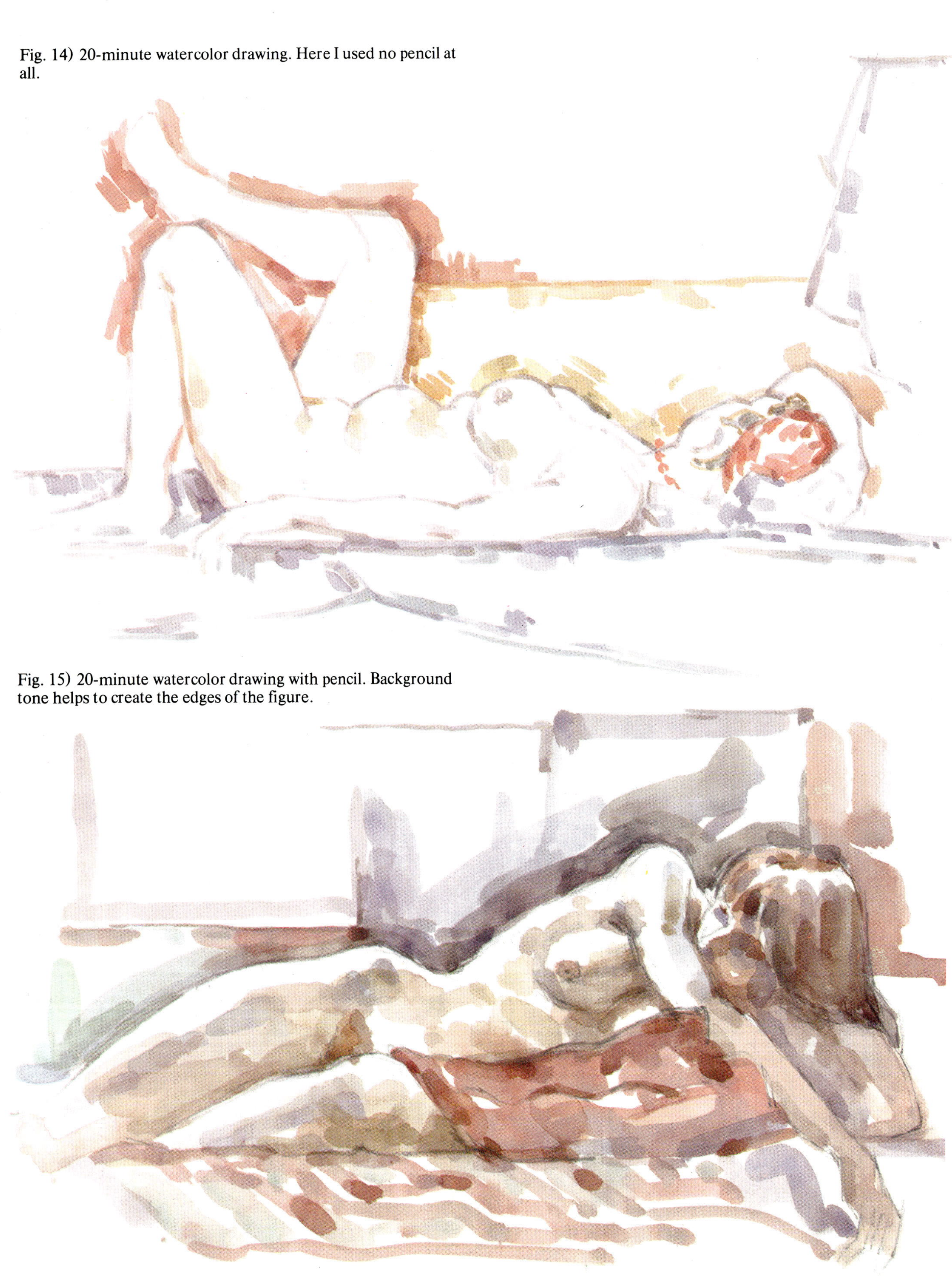

Fig. 15) 20-minute watercolor drawing with pencil. Background tone helps to create the edges of the figure.

of wash, overlaying it several times during the building-up process. This drawing took two hours to complete—time enough to produce a finished and well-studied work.

I drew each of the other figures in this section from a short pose of not more than 20 minutes. For these I used the small pocket box. Because these drawings needed relatively small amounts of watercolor, the mixing area in the box lid was sufficient. In each case, my intention was to capture the overall character of the pose, rather than to make a thorough and detailed study.

Figure 14 was drawn without adding pencil. In this case, I wanted to depict the shape of the figure entirely with the brush. I varied the color to emphasize certain shapes.

In figure 15 I worked at creating the edge of the figure by building up background tones. Without this darkened background, the smooth, white quality of the model's skin would have been lost.

I drew the figures on this page from 15-minute poses. I used pencil in figure 16 to sharpen and define the edges. In figure 17 I was more interested in shape than in tone, so I drew with only watercolor and brush.

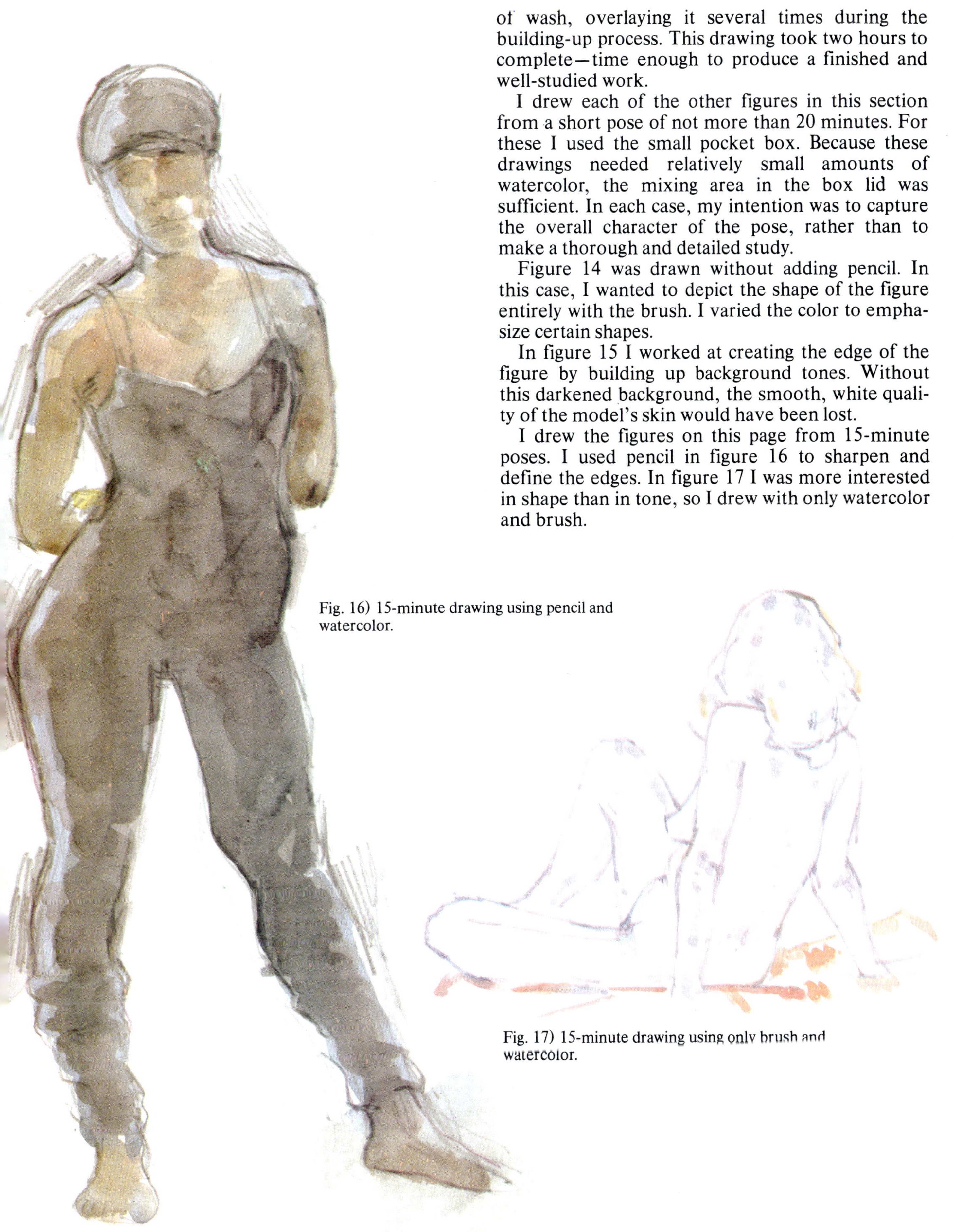

Fig. 16) 15-minute drawing using pencil and watercolor.

Fig. 17) 15-minute drawing using only brush and watercolor.

Using Oil, Acrylic And Gouache

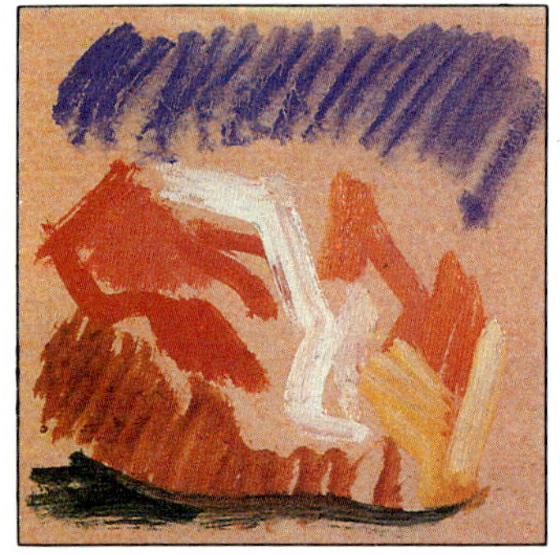

OIL

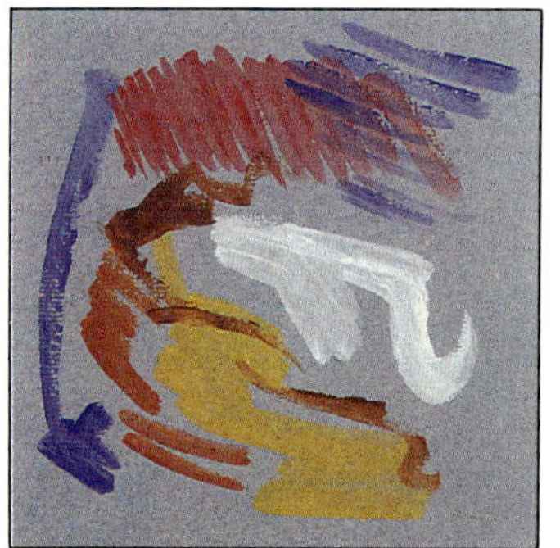

ACRYLIC

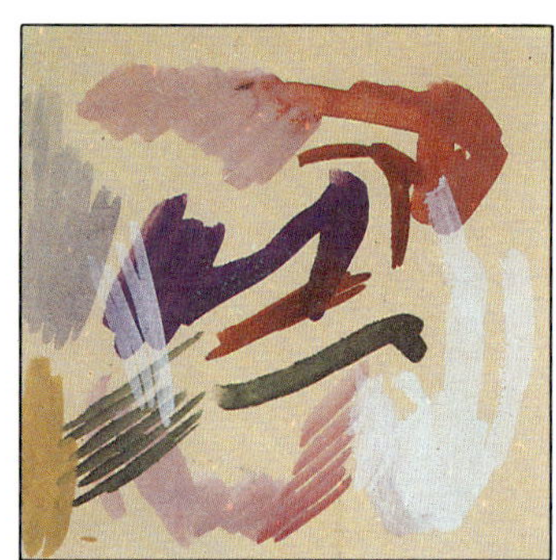

GOUACHE

Oil, acrylic and gouache are all opaque paints. Watercolor, in contrast, is transparent. The fundamental difference between watercolor and the other three media is the way you get light colors. Watercolor is diluted with water on white paper. Oil, acrylic and gouache are typically lightened with white of the same medium.

You might think that these opaque media, so obviously used for painting, are not well-suited to the practice of drawing the figure. But I believe that oil, acrylic and gouache will provide you with flexible and powerful means of expression. French painter Edgar Degas, already discussed in the section on pastels, is also well known for innovative studies of dancers in which he used thinned oil paint on paper.

SOME BASICS

If you have ever used a brush to draw with, you know the special feeling it gives. Drawing with a brush usually involves the whole arm rather than just the wrist, and this tends to produce bold and expressive images. When you draw with a brush, you will probably find yourself simplifying more than you would with pencil or pastels. You will also group areas of contour in a stronger way. Finally, of course, you will be able to use the brush to indicate tone or shadow.

One of the distinct advantages of these opaque media is the use of white or other light colors to achieve particular effects. In the acrylic drawing on the opposite page, I have used white to increase the silhouette quality of the legs. In addition, I was able to paint over unneeded lines with white. You can see that in drawings such as these, a light color can be used to construct, rather than to merely decorate.

How much color should you use in an oil, acrylic or gouache drawing? You should be guided by what you feel each drawing or study needs to enhance certain aspects. For the studies of the dancer on the opposite page, I used relatively few colors. My intention was to apply color in a local and somewhat descriptive way, rather than to create a full painting. I used black, red, blue, yellow and white—the three primary colors, plus darkening and lightening colors.

In the drawings in oil and gouache on pages 46 and 47, I used color to obtain flesh tones. White in these drawings was used principally to produce various subtle versions of the pink and yellow tints found in flesh.

The gouache drawing also makes use of color in a more decorative way. Without the splash of color seen in the leg warmers, the three figures might have formed too large an area of unbroken flesh tones. Notice how in quite a few places the neutral gray of the paper shows through. In these areas I used only a light application of the gouache, or none at all.

I'll now discuss each of the three opaque media in some detail.

OIL

In most cases, you will draw with oil paint on canvas or board. But you can also use oil paint on paper, if the paper is properly treated. It's a good idea to prepare several sheets in advance, so there is always a surface to work on when you need it.

The oil drawing on page 46 was done on heavy writing paper. The paper was thoroughly sized with two coats of a mixture of cold water and caesin glue. The surface was then toned down to green with acrylic paint. The result was a non-greasy surface that was ready to be painted in oil. Acrylic can always be used this way as a *primer* or *underpainting* for oil—but never the other way around.

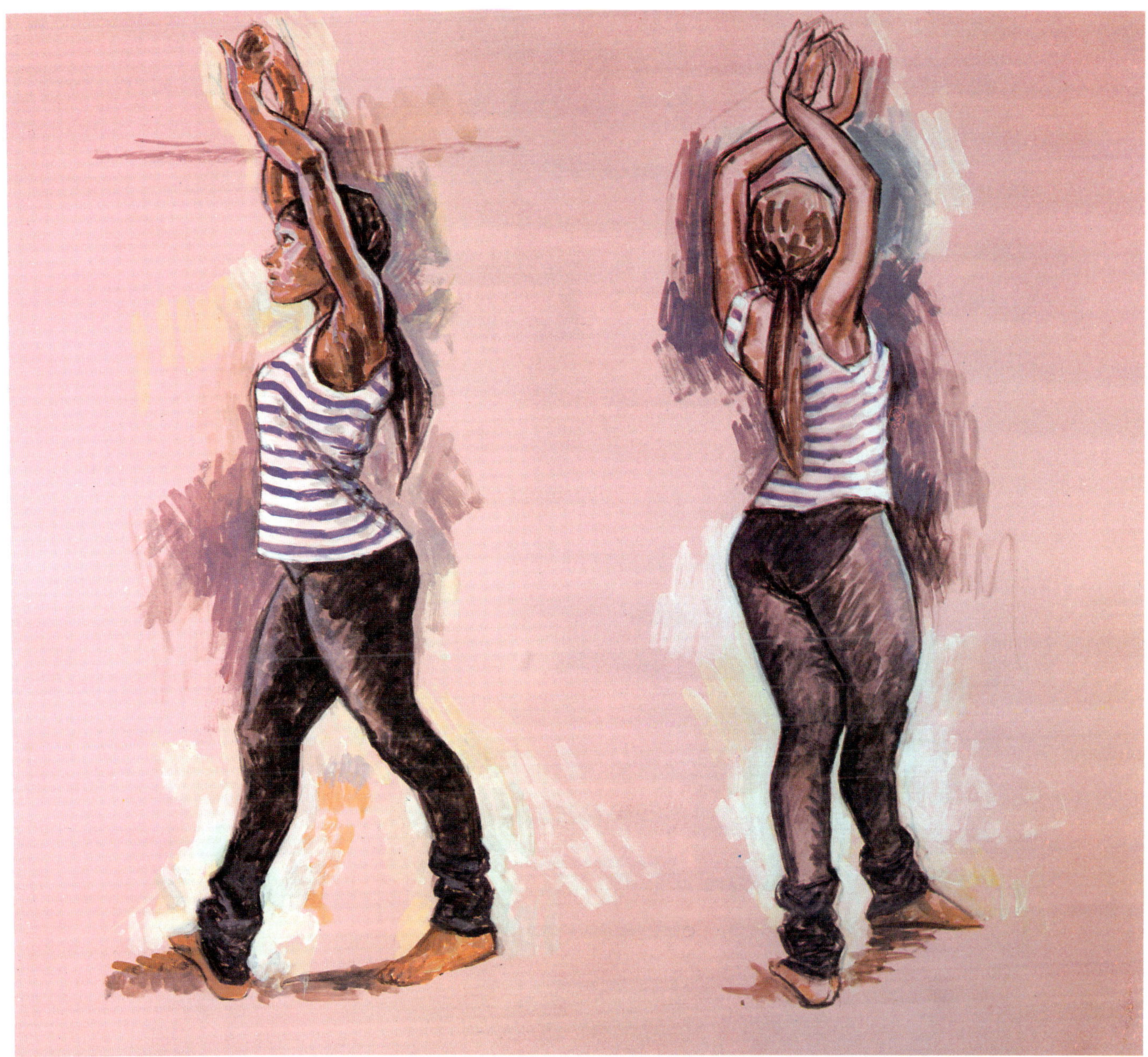

Acrylic drawing.

You'll find that the big disadvantage to using oil paint for figure drawing is the amount of equipment needed. Obviously, if the pose is only for an hour, you don't want to waste time squeezing colors out of tubes and thinning paints. The moral of the story is to *be prepared* if you use oil paint for figure drawing.

ACRYLIC

Like colored pencils, acrylics are a relatively recent invention. This paint uses a synthetic resin to bind pigment. Unlike oil paint, it is water-based. This gives it extreme flexibility. You can apply acrylic paints in thick, opaque mixes like oil paints, or in thin washes like watercolors. The paint dries very quickly and is then waterproof.

Acrylics are easier to use than oil paints. You can paint directly onto paper that has not been primed or sized. And you need only water to clean acrylic paint from your brushes. You should remember, though, that the paint will form a skin and dry quickly once it is out of the tube. Be careful not to leave acrylic paint too long on your palette.

GOUACHE

Gouache has a pastel-like quality. It is opaque like oil and acrylic paint, but is not waterproof when dry. This means that you cannot lay new colors over a

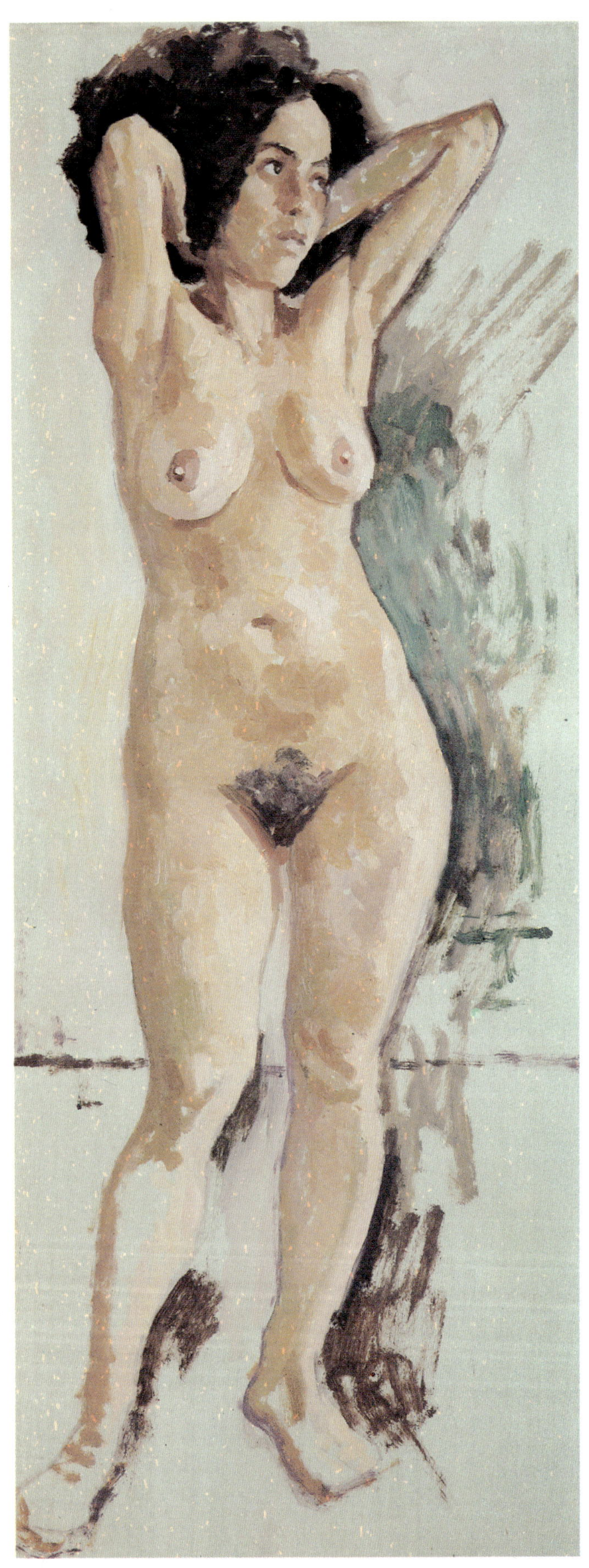

previously painted surface to the extent that you would with the other two media.

You can use gouache on paper or on mounting card. Like oil and acrylics, gouache is particularly effective on a toned surface. The color of the surface allows you to place light and dark colors side by side. You can see this effect in the drawing on page 47.

Gouache has a tendency to change to a slightly different color when it dries. The degree of the change depends on the thickness of the paint, and on how much paint there already is on the drawing surface. Once you have practiced with this medium and become familiar with the changes, you won't find this such an irritating quality.

Like acrylic paint, gouache takes only a few minutes to dry. If your colors dry on the palette, though, you can wet and re-use them much as you would with watercolor.

Left: Oil drawing.

Opposite: Gouache drawing. The color breaks up the large areas of flesh tones.

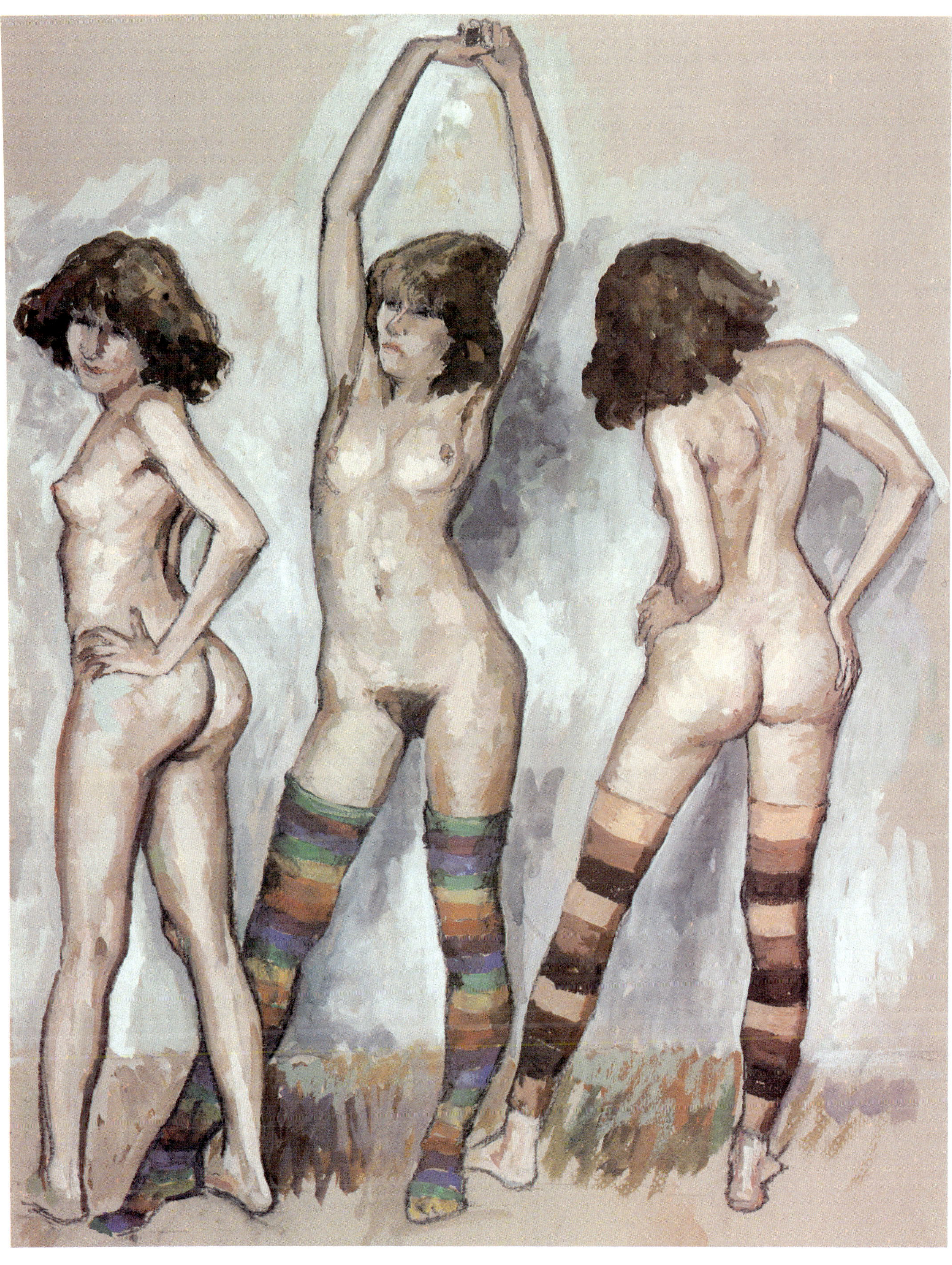

Mixed Media

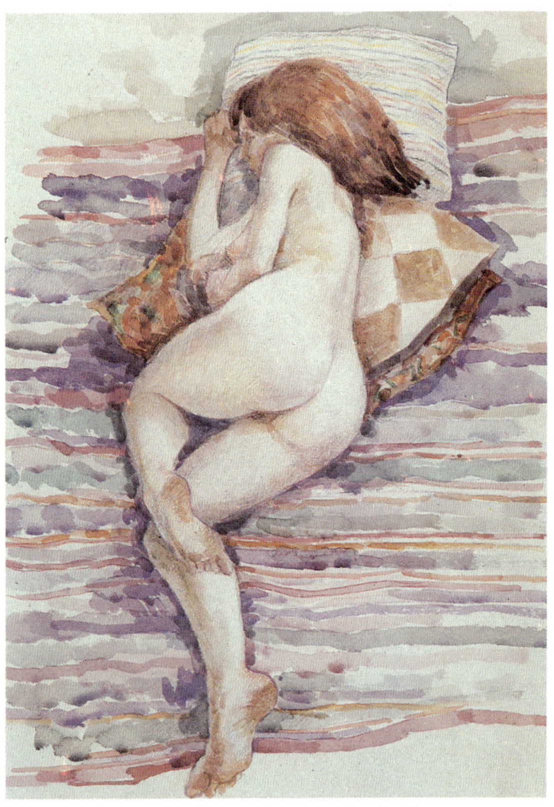

Drawing in watercolor and colored pencils.

Figure drawing is often taken as a serious and academic study. Without denying that aspect of it, I believe that enjoyment and experimentation are just as relevant.

LEARN TO EXPERIMENT

The medium you choose for a drawing plays an important role in more than the obvious, visible ways. That is, the medium you are working in actually affects your thought process while you draw. This is why I encourage you to try many different types of media. In every case, you will observe a difference in your creative process in addition to the finished product.

It is just as important to see what happens when you mix media in a drawing. You might want to do this because a mixed-media effect was your goal from the start. But it's more likely that the drawing itself, as it progresses, will demand the introduction of a new medium.

For example, you might begin a drawing in red chalk. When you find that some areas have become too red, you can use white chalk or pastel to highlight certain areas. Or, if you want to make the image denser, you can introduce black ink. Obviously, you can see that one way to keep a drawing going is to change the medium each time an area becomes saturated or overworked.

SOME EFFECTIVE COMBINATIONS

I like the combination of some types of paint and pencil. By combining media such as these, you can explore *texture* in a drawing. The drawing above was done in watercolor and colored pencils. Colored pencil sits very well on top a watercolor wash in the form of a cross-hatching technique. Rather than two single layers, I alternated layers of wash and pencil.

Colored pencils are about 85% waterproof. This means that when you lay a wash over pencil lines, the edges will soften slightly. I like this attractive effect. But if you want sharp and well-defined lines, use the pencil last.

Remember to consider the drawing surface when you combine media. In this drawing, the white paper plays an important role in showing the body's luminosity. I wanted to show the porcelain-like qual-

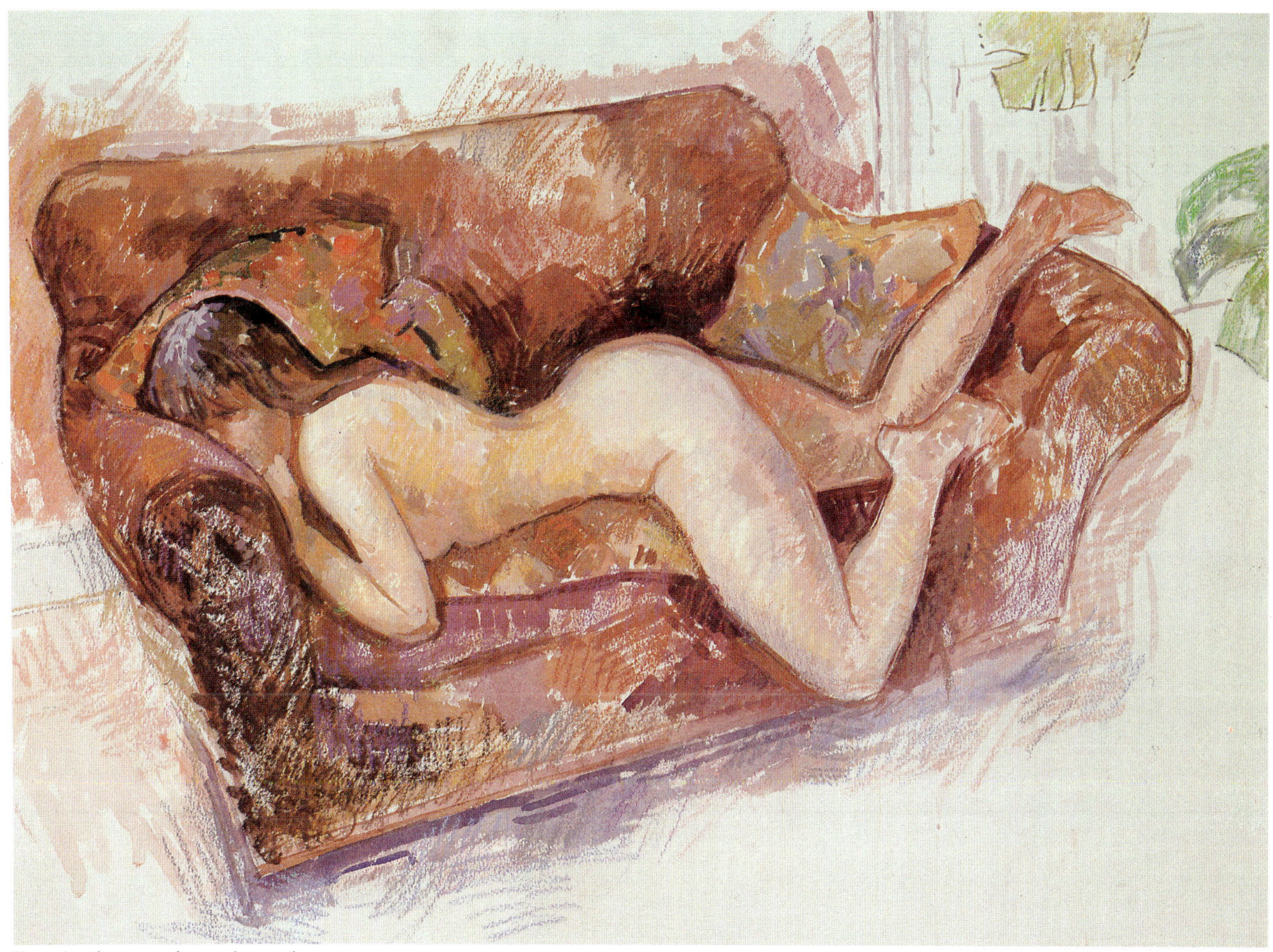

Drawing in gouache and pastels.

ity of the model's skin. For this I found the delicate over-laying of wash and colored pencils suitable. The striped background material helped to emphasize her pale and delicate tones.

The drawing on this page was done in gouache and pastels. Here, too, I was exploring possible textures. The greater covering power of these two media creates a very different effect from that of the previous drawing.

You can achieve various effects with pastel, depending on the stage at which it is introduced. By the time pastel has been applied to the surface, it has become almost pure pigment. This means that if you put a brush with water or paint across the surface, the pastel pigment will dissolve. The pigment is then like paint—and you can move it around on the paper as you desire.

In the drawing above I applied some pastel that was then dissolved with a brush. But here I was mostly interested in the textures created by applying pastel across an area already painted with gouache. For this, I used similar colors in the two media.

In both drawings, the color surrounding the figure was important. I believe that the best way to express the pale luminosity of the body is to contrast it with a dark, richly colored background. This is most effective when you use white paper.

Anatomy For The Artist

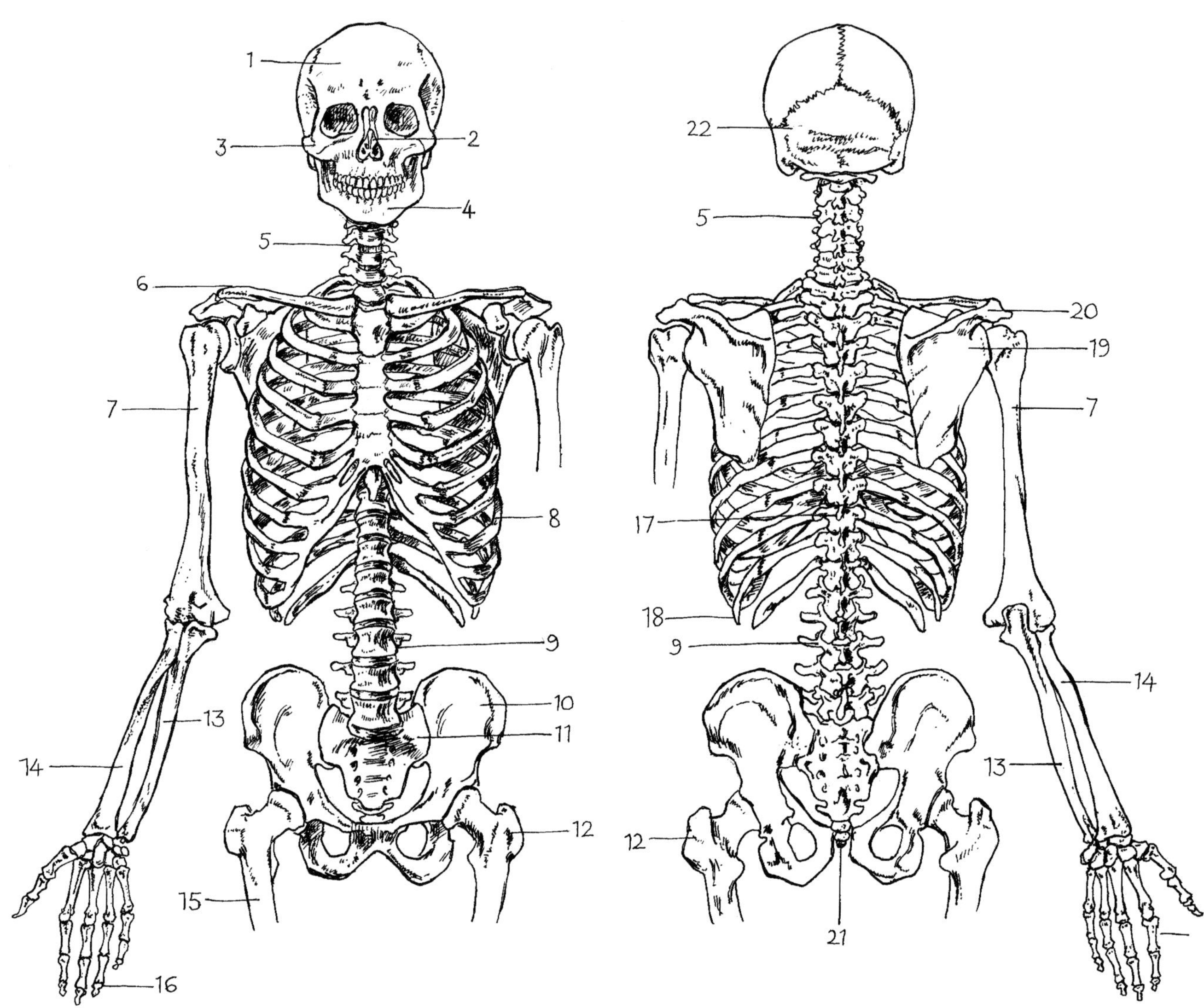

In the majority of this book I discuss drawing from a nude figure. Therefore it is appropriate to include a brief survey of human anatomy. This is a complex subject, and each artist studies it to whatever degree he feels is necessary. In this section I give just an introduction and some basic information on bones and muscles.

WHY STUDY ANATOMY?

Do you need to know anatomy to become a good figurative artist? Not necessarily. A person skilled in drawing can cope with any situation, but I believe that a knowledge of anatomy *can* be useful.

Very often, drawing problems that seem unsolvable can be reasoned out by applying your knowledge of anatomy. For example, imagine you were asked

Bones of the head, thorax and arm:

1) Frontal bone
2) Nasal bone
3) Zygomatic arch
4) Mandible
5) Cervical vertebrae (7)
6) Clavicle
7) Humerus
8) Rib cage
9) Lumbar vertebrae (5)
10) Iliac bone
11) Sacrum
12) Great trochanter of femur
13) Ulna
14) Radius
15) Femur
16) Bones of the hand
17) Dorsal vertebrae (12)
18) Floating ribs (4)
19) Scapula
20) Acromion
21) Coccyx
22) Occipital

to draw a boat. The drawing would have a greater certainty about it if you first studied the construction of sailing vessels. That knowledge of technical details would help you draw the boat with more assurance and conviction.

The same principle applies to drawing the human body. Of course, you should always draw what you see rather than what you know. But knowing what lies underneath the surface can help you understand and express what you see.

As you read the following sections, follow the numbered diagrams on the corresponding pages.

THE SKELETON

We'll begin our survey of human anatomy with the skeleton. The skeleton is the frame on which everything in the body rests. It has evolved to give maximum mobility and stability to the movements we perform.

Torso—The spine forms the central part of the structure. It supports the skull and twelve pairs of ribs. The ribs provide protection for the lungs and other internal organs. When it reaches the pelvis, the spine rests and divides the body weight evenly onto the legs. This allows many complex movements from the waist upward while the feet are planted firmly on the ground.

The pelvis is the part of the skeleton that shows the greatest difference between the sexes. The female pelvis is wide and shallow. There is a greater distance between the *coccyx* at the base of the spine and the *pubic arch.* This causes the characteristic wider hips in women. It is important to study this area in standing poses. You should work at getting the correct angle across the hips.

Legs and Feet—The weight resting on the pelvis is then transmitted onto the *femur* bones of the upper legs. The femur is the longest and strongest bone in the whole body. It connects to the pelvis by means of a ball-and-socket joint. This joint is much deeper than the similar ball-and-socket joint of the shoulder. Therefore, it is more stable and less mobile then the shoulder joint.

The junction at the knee consists of the femur resting on top of the *tibia,* the main bone of the lower leg. At the front of the patella, connected only by ligaments, is a small bone called the *patella.* This is what we know as the *kneecap.* The patella can only move backward and forward. The long narrow bone running alongside the tibia is the *fibula.* At its lower end, the fibula forms the ankle.

The foot is made up of various small bones called *tarsals* and *metatarsals.* In each of the toes are three *phalanges.* The big toe, however, has only two phalanges.

Shoulders, Arms and Hands—In the upper skeleton, shoulders are formed by the *clavicle,* or collarbone, in front and the *scapula* at the back. This is another area of the skeleton where a marked difference between the sexes is apparent. Male shoulders are generally wider than female shoulders.

The arms and hands perform the most complex body movements. This is due entirely to their structure. The *humerus*—the only bone of the upper arm—is joined to the scapula of the shoulder. As I mentioned earlier, this junction is a shallow, ball-and-socket joint. The relative shallowness of the joint allows for great mobility in the arm.

Two bones, the *ulna* and the *radius,* extend from the elbow to the wrist. The radius crosses the ulna and then joins the bones of the wrist and hand.

The wrist is formed of many small bones. The hand, similar to the foot in structure, has five bones

Bones of the leg and foot:
1) Femur
2) Patella
3) Tibia
4) Fibula
5) Talus
6) Great trochanter of femur
7) Pelvis
8) Sacrum
9) Navicular
10) Calcaneus
11) Cuboid
12) Bones of the foot

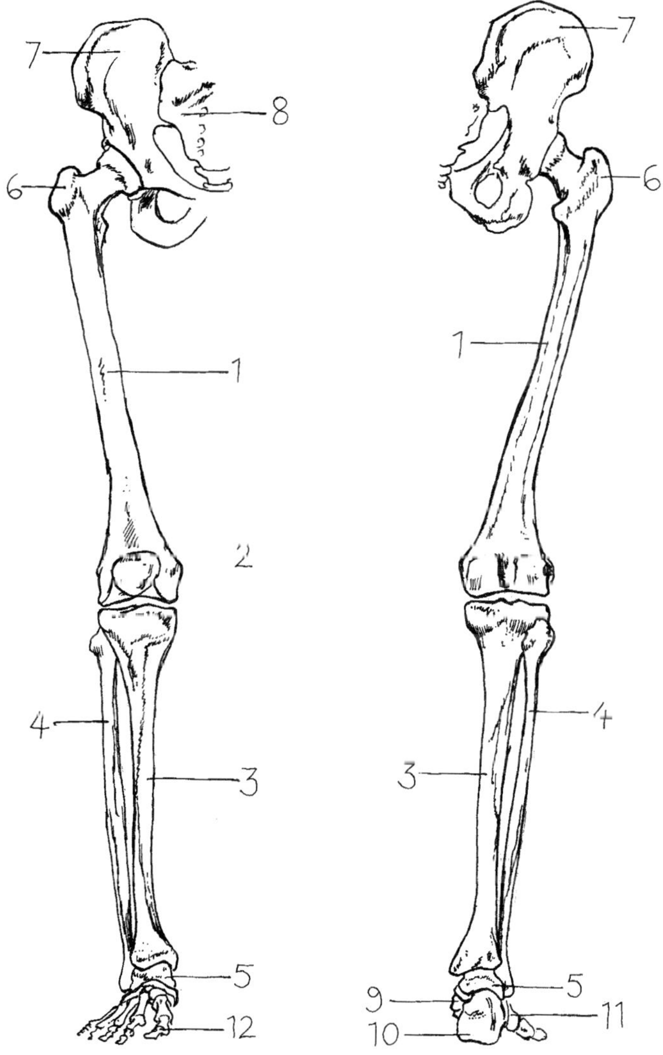

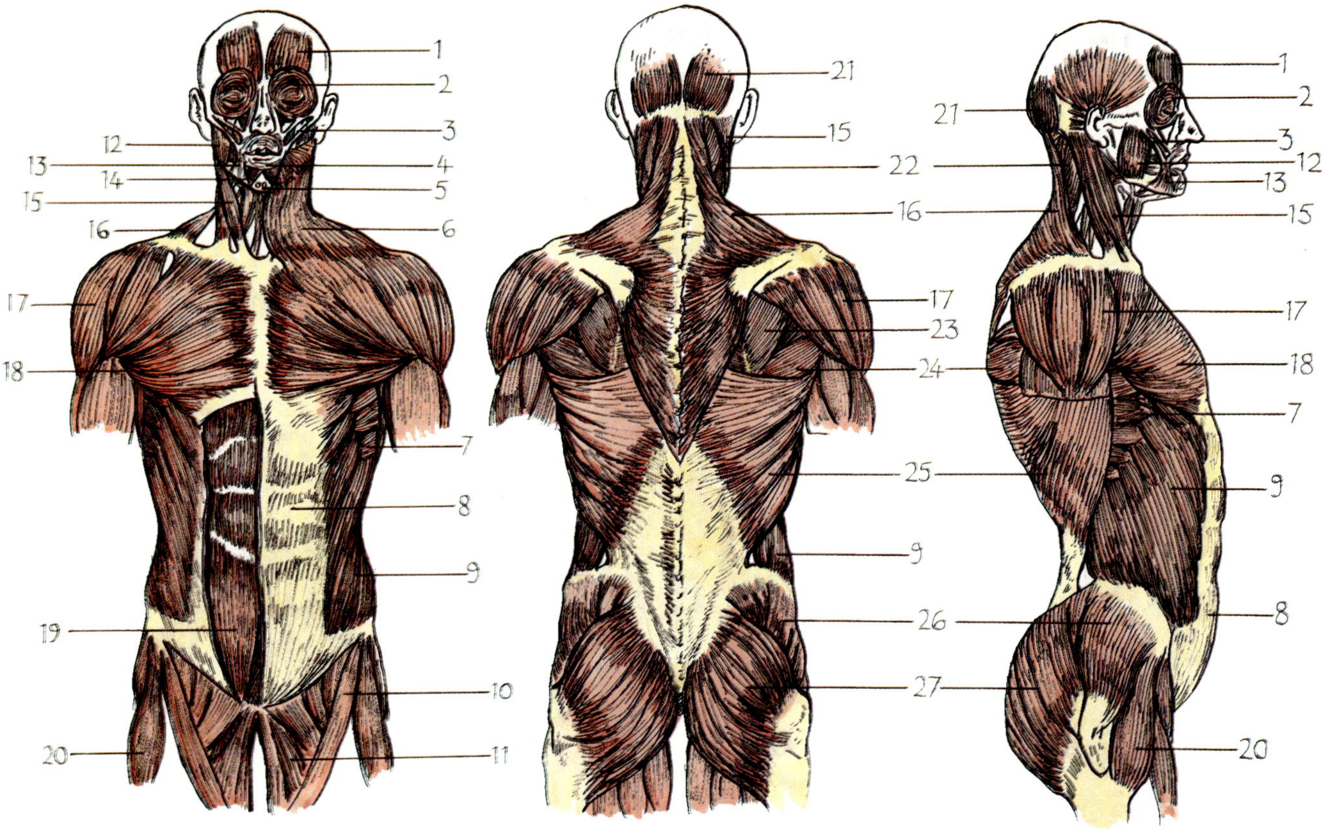

Muscles of the head, neck and trunk:

1) Frontalis
2) Orbicularis of the eye
3) Zygomaticus major and minor
4) Orbicularis of the mouth
5) Mentalis
6) Platysma
7) Serratus anterior
8) Aponeurosis covering the rectus abdominis
9) External oblique
10) Sartorius
11) Adductor longus
12) Masseter
13) Depressor of the angle of the mouth
14) Elevator of the chin
15) Sternomastoid
16) Trapezius
17) Deltoid
18) Pectoralis major
19) Rectus abdominis
20) Tensor fasciae latae
21) Occipitalis
22) Splenius capitis
23) Infraspinatus
24) Teres major
25) Latissimus dorsi
26) Gluteus medius
27) Gluteus maximus

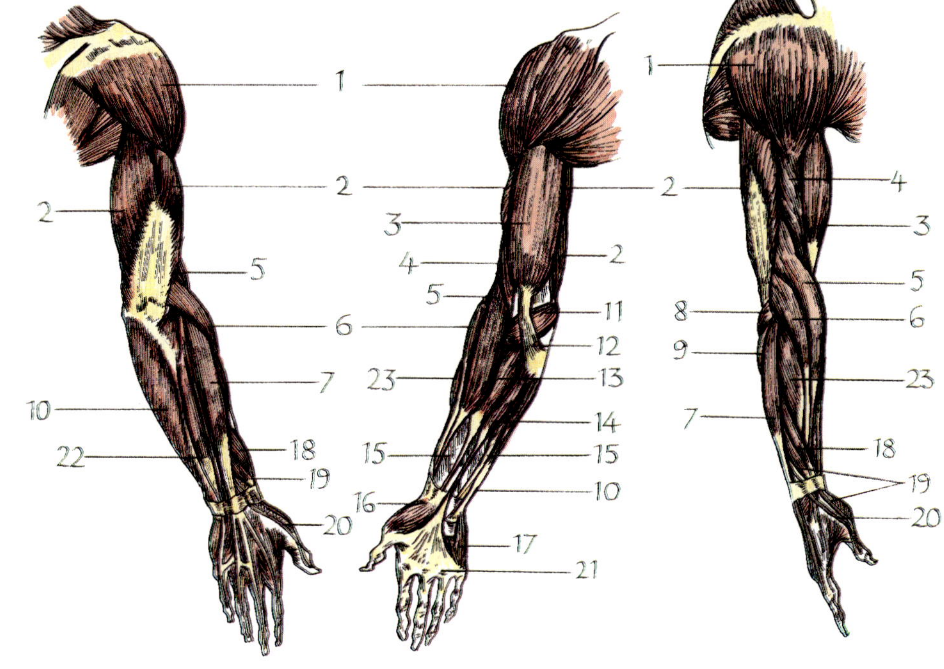

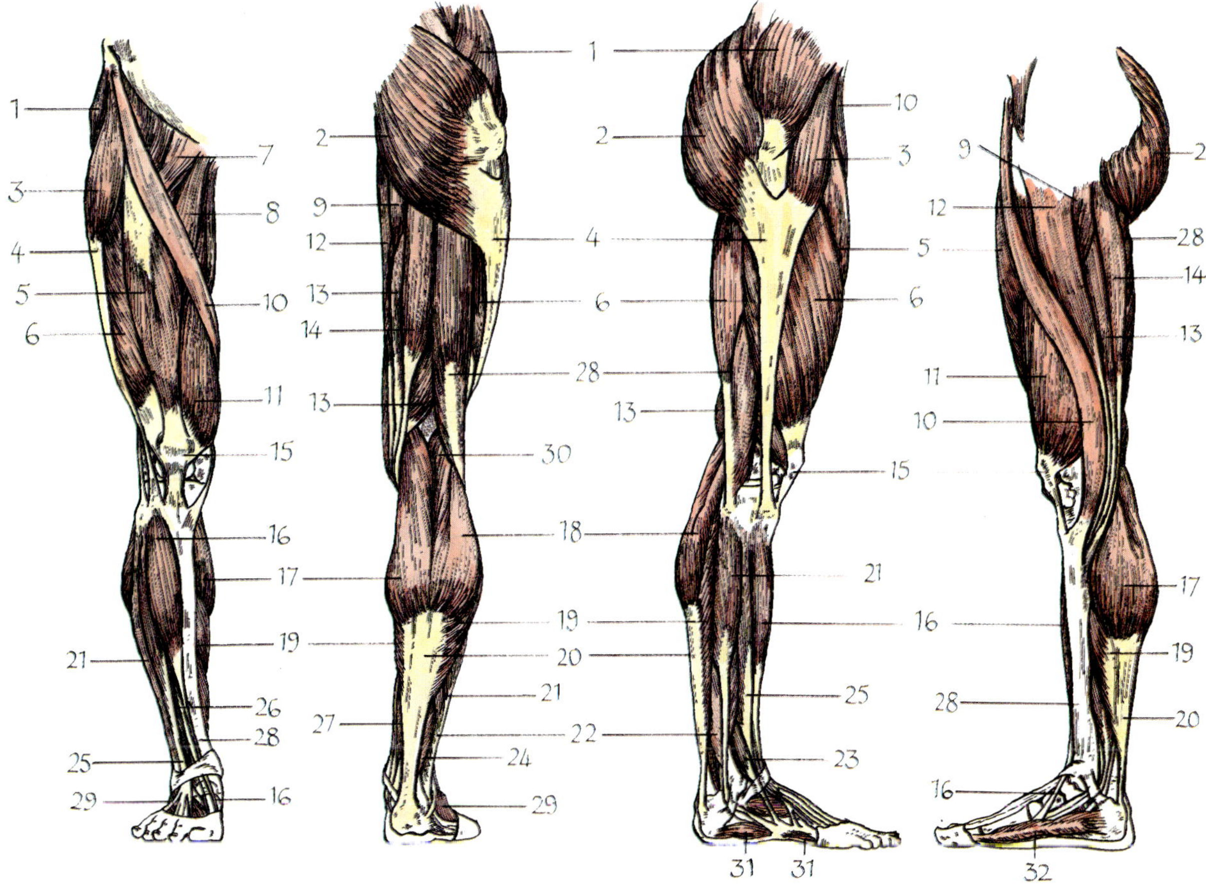

Muscles of the arm:
1) Deltoid
2) Triceps
3) Biceps
4) Brachialis
5) Brachioradialis
6) Extensor carpi radialis longus
7) Extensor digitorum
8) Anconeus
9) Extensor carpi ulnaris
10) Flexor carpi ulnaris
11) Pronater teres
12) Tendon extension of biceps
13) Flexor carpi radialis
14) Palmaris longus
15) Flexor digitorum superficialis
16) Muscles of the thumb eminence
17) Muscles of the little finger eminence
18) Abductor pollocis longus
19) Extensor pollocis brevis (tendon of the thumb)
20) Extensor pollocis longus (tendon of the thumb)
21) Palmar fascia
22) Extensor carpi ulnaris
23) Extensor carpi radialis brevis

Muscles of the leg:
1) Gluteus medius
2) Gluteus maximus
3) Tensor fasciae latae
4) Ilio tibial band
5) Rectus femoris
6) Vastus lateralis
7) Pectineus
8) Adductor longus
9) Adductor magnus
10) Sartorius
11) Vastus medialis
12) Gracilis
13) Semimembranosus
14) Semitendinosus
15) Patella
16) Tibialis anterior
17) Gastrocnemius—inner head
18) Gastrocnemius—outer head
19) Soleus
20) Achilles tendon
21) Peroneus longus
22) Peroneus brevis
23) Peroneus tertius
24) Flexor hallucis longus
25) Extensor digitorum longus
26) Extensor hallucis longus
27) Flexor digitorum longus
28) Biceps femoris
29) Extensor digitorum brevis
30) Plantaris
31) Abductor digiti minimi
32) Abductor hallucis

called *metacarpals.* Each finger has three *phalanxes,* except the thumb, which has two.

MUSCLES

Within our brief survey of human anatomy, there is not room to discuss each muscle and its movements in detail. But you'll learn about the main muscle groups and their functions. As before, my purpose is to show you what may improve your skill in drawing the human body. Refer to the corresponding diagrams on pages 52 through 55 as you read.

When you look at the body, the muscles you can see will depend on the person's degree of fitness. In an overweight person, very few muscles are visible. But even in the thinnest person, there is a layer of fatty tissue known as the *panniculus adiposus.* This fatty layer covers the entire body. It masks the actual form of the muscles.

Muscles generally work in groups. This is another reason why it is difficult to trace the movement of an individual muscle. You need to study the underlying structure in order to gain a fuller understanding of muscles.

Muscles occur in two basic forms. The first is long and narrow, but often thick. It is found mainly in the arms and legs. The second form is wide and sheet-like. These muscles occur mainly in the torso.

Neck and Torso—A very important muscle called

the *sternomastoid* joins the head to the shoulders. This muscle is normally visible under the skin. It runs diagonally from just behind the ear around to the collar bone. This forms what we call the *pit* of the neck.

The *trapezius* runs from the collarbone near the outer edge of the shoulders, up the back of the neck to the skull.

The wide, thin muscles of the torso provide added protection for the internal organs. At the front of the torso is a large muscle called the *rectus abdominus.* This muscle connects the rib cage to the pelvis. It is the principle muscle used in sit-up exercises. The rectus abdominus is usually visible under the skin, even if it is accompanied by much fat.

On the side of the torso are two important muscles called the *external oblique* and the *serratus anterior.* The serratus is higher and connects to the scapula, the bone that forms the back of the shoulder. Many arm movements are aided by the serratus.

Deep muscles of the back:
1) Splenius capitis
2) Levator scapulae
3) Rhomboideus
4) Erector spinae
5) Serratus posterior

Muscles of the arm:
1) Deltoid
2) Triceps
3) Biceps
4) Extensor digitorum
5) Extensor carpi radialis longus
6) Ulna
7) Radius
8) Extensor carpi ulnaris

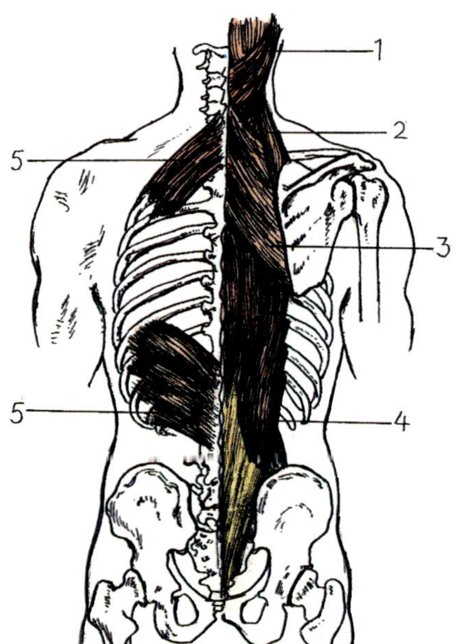

Back—A group of deep-lying muscles called the *erector spinae* run along the spinal column. These muscles extend from the *cervical vertebrae* at the neck to the *lumbar vertebrae* at the pelvis. Erector spinae give the back its characteristic furrow in the center.

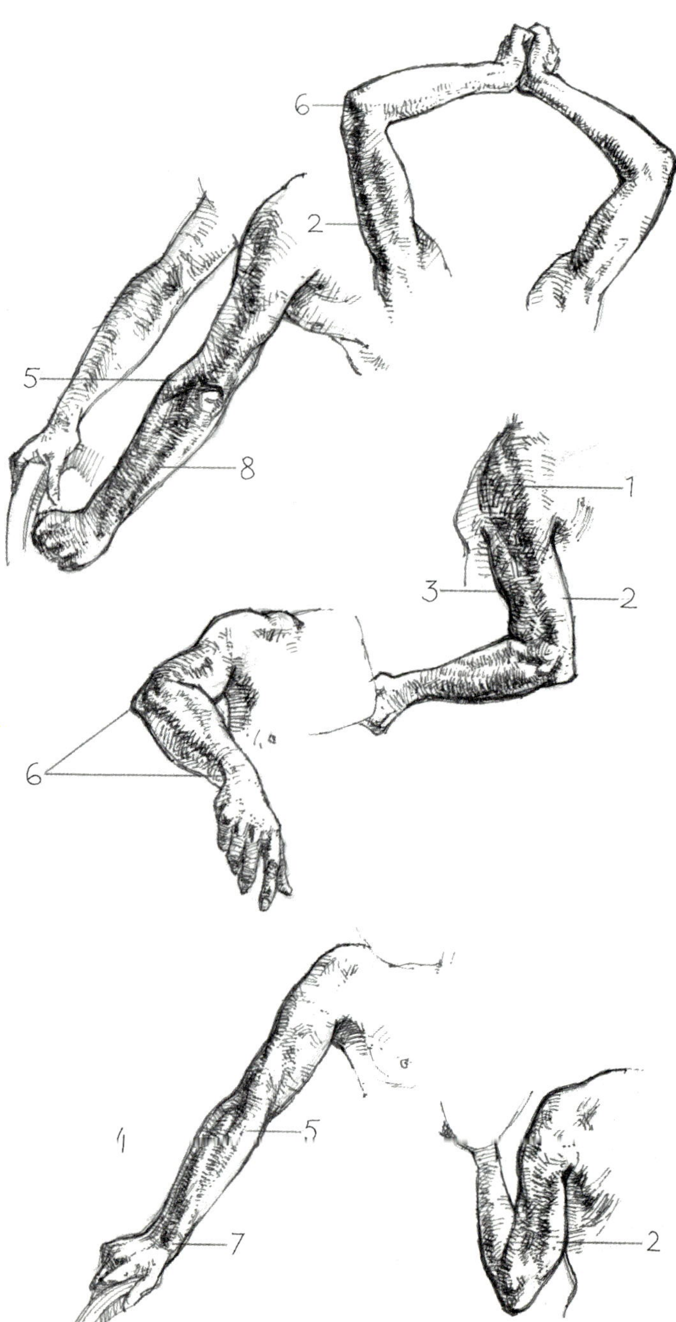

Another set of muscles lies over the erector spinae—the *latissimus dorsi* and the *trapezius.* They are very broad and thin and lie close to the surface. The *latissimus dorsi* covers practically the entire back. At the armpit it joins the *pectoralis major,* which is the major chest muscle.

Shoulders, Arms and Hands—The other important muscle in the shoulder area is the *deltoid.* This is a triangle-shaped muscle covering the top of the arm just below the shoulder. The deltoid is a powerful muscle. It governs most whole-arm movements.

In the upper arm are two major muscles covering the humerus bone. These are strong muscles called the *biceps* and *triceps.* They connect to the scapula of the shoulder and to the radius and ulna of the forearm. These muscles direct many forearm movements.

In the lower part of the arm are many long, thin muscles. These connect to the fingers and thumb by tendons. They combine to produce a bulky shape before tapering into the wrist. This gives the forearm its characteristic shape.

Of this group of lower-arm muscles, two are particularly important. The *brachioradialis* and the *extensor carpi radialis longus* lift the forearm with a crane-like action.

Legs and Feet—Leg muscles resemble arm muscles. In the upper leg, muscles are thicker and stronger for moving the entire limb. Below the knee the muscles are thinner. They taper into tendons that connect to and move the toes.

At the back and top of the legs is the powerful *gluteus maximus* muscle. This forms the main muscle of the buttock, and is used to power running and jumping. The buttock area is more liable to collect fat than most other areas of the body. Because of this, the underlying muscles can be seen only on an athletic person.

The *hamstrings* are large tendons that form the back of the knee. Several muscles from the thigh area join to form these tendons. One group of muscles runs from the lower part of the pelvis down the whole length of the femur. The *sartorius* is a major muscle in this area. It extends diagonally from the pelvis to the hamstring, to form the basic character of the upper leg.

Three other muscles join in a common tendon called the *ilio tibial band.* It runs down the side of the leg to the lower knee. These muscles are the *gluteus maximus, the gluteus medius* and the *tensor fasciae latae.*

The area we call the *calf* is made up principally of the *gastrocnemius* muscle. It is divided into two parts, called the *inner head* and the *outer head.* These connect to the femur of the upper leg. Together with the hamstrings, the gastrocnemius forms a powerful junction that operates the entire lower leg.

At its lower end, the gastrocnemius becomes a tendon. This is the familiar Achilles tendon. It attaches to the heel bone and performs many of the main foot movements.

At the front of the lower leg, the tibia bone lies just under the surface. This is one of the three areas where a major bone can be observed just below the skin. The other two areas are the collar bone and the crest of the pelvis.

Finally, the *peroneal* group of muscles forms the area around the ankle. These muscles contribute to the movements of the foot. Like the hand, the foot has very little flesh. It is made up mostly of bones and the tendons that attach to them.

All muscles have a fleshy part that expands and contracts in response to brain signals. The fleshy part is joined to a tendon, which does the actual pushing or pulling. In the diagrams of muscles in this section, I have colored the fleshy parts red and the tendons yellow.

Muscles of the leg:
1) Tensor fasciae latae
2) Biceps femoris
3) Soleus
4) Peroneus longus
5) Tibialis anterior
6) Vastus lateralis
7) Achilles tendon
8) Gastrocnemius

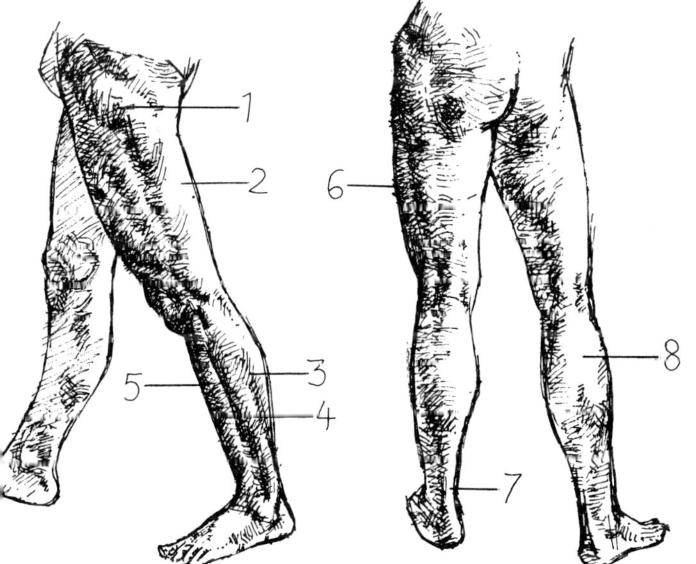

Head, Hands And Feet

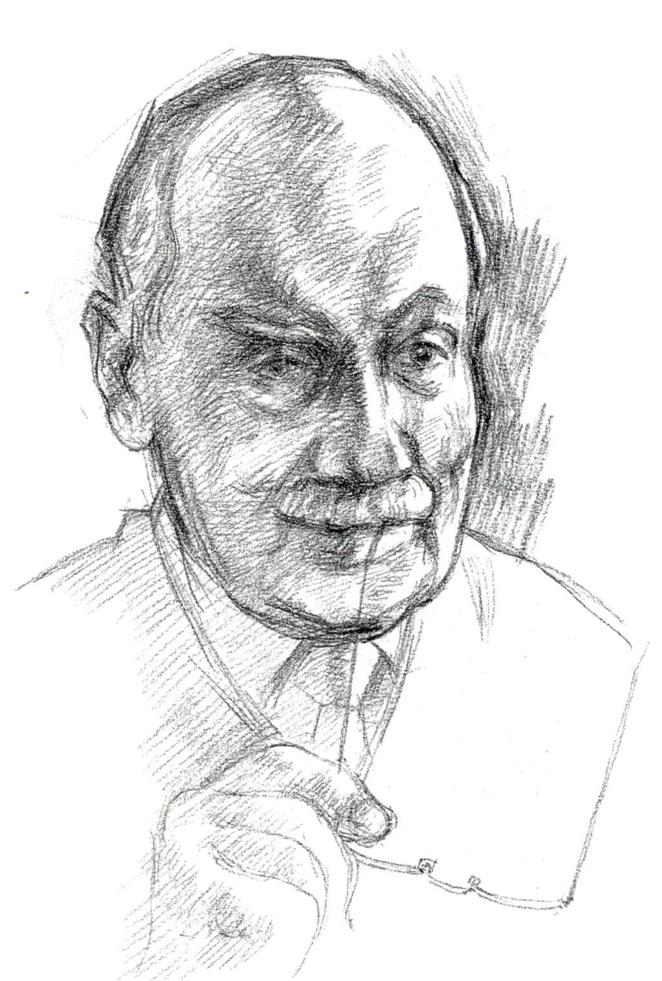

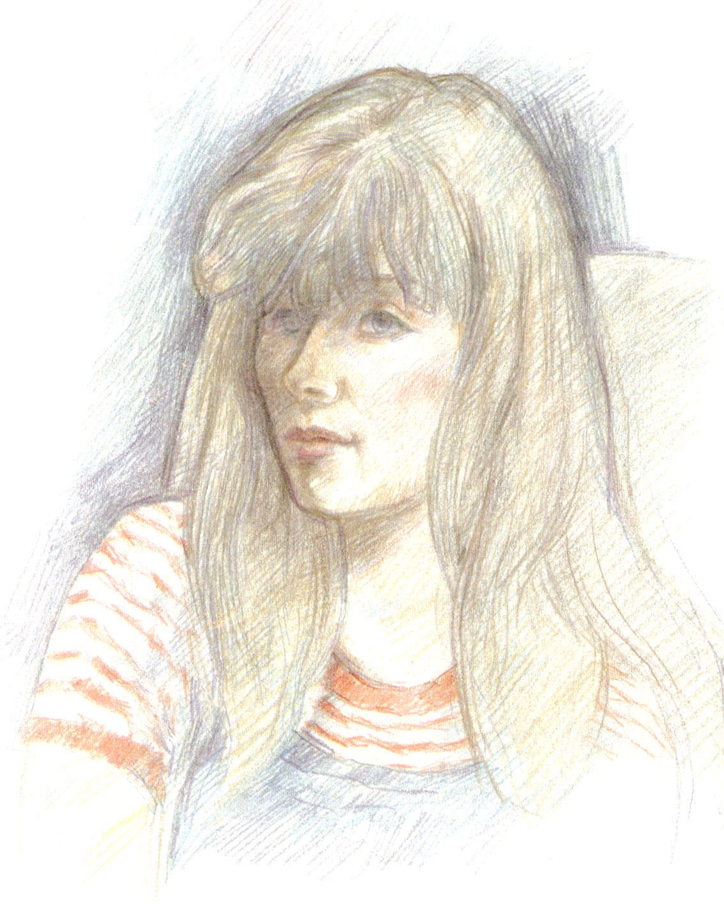

Left: Chalk drawing.

Above: Colored-pencil drawing.

The head, hands and feet are body parts that many people have difficulty drawing. The head, of course, presents a special challenge in portrait drawing and painting. But there is no reason for you to have trouble with any of these areas in figure drawing.

Remember that when you are drawing from life in the studio, you can concentrate on the figure as a whole. None of the extremities requires excessive attention. Especially when the scale of the drawing is small, you can greatly simplify these areas.

It's true, though, that the head and hands in particular express much of a person's individual character. Here I discuss some points for you to bear in mind while drawing head and hands.

HEAD

The chalk drawing above of an elderly man shows a face with plenty of character. When you do a study of this sort, be sure to place the subject's head in good light. Try to position the light to provide the most sympathetic view of the face. And if you are drawing an older person such as this one, don't overemphasize the wrinkles.

Remember that overall shape, structure and proportion are important. Take note of the distance from the top of the head to the eyebrow. Then note the length of the nose and the distance from nose to chin. Pay special attention to the angles of eyebrows and ears. These can also convey much of the subject's character.

Notice that in the colored-pencil drawing of the girl, the entire form is much smoother and tighter. These subtle changes of plane are more suitable for expressing the appearance and character of a young person.

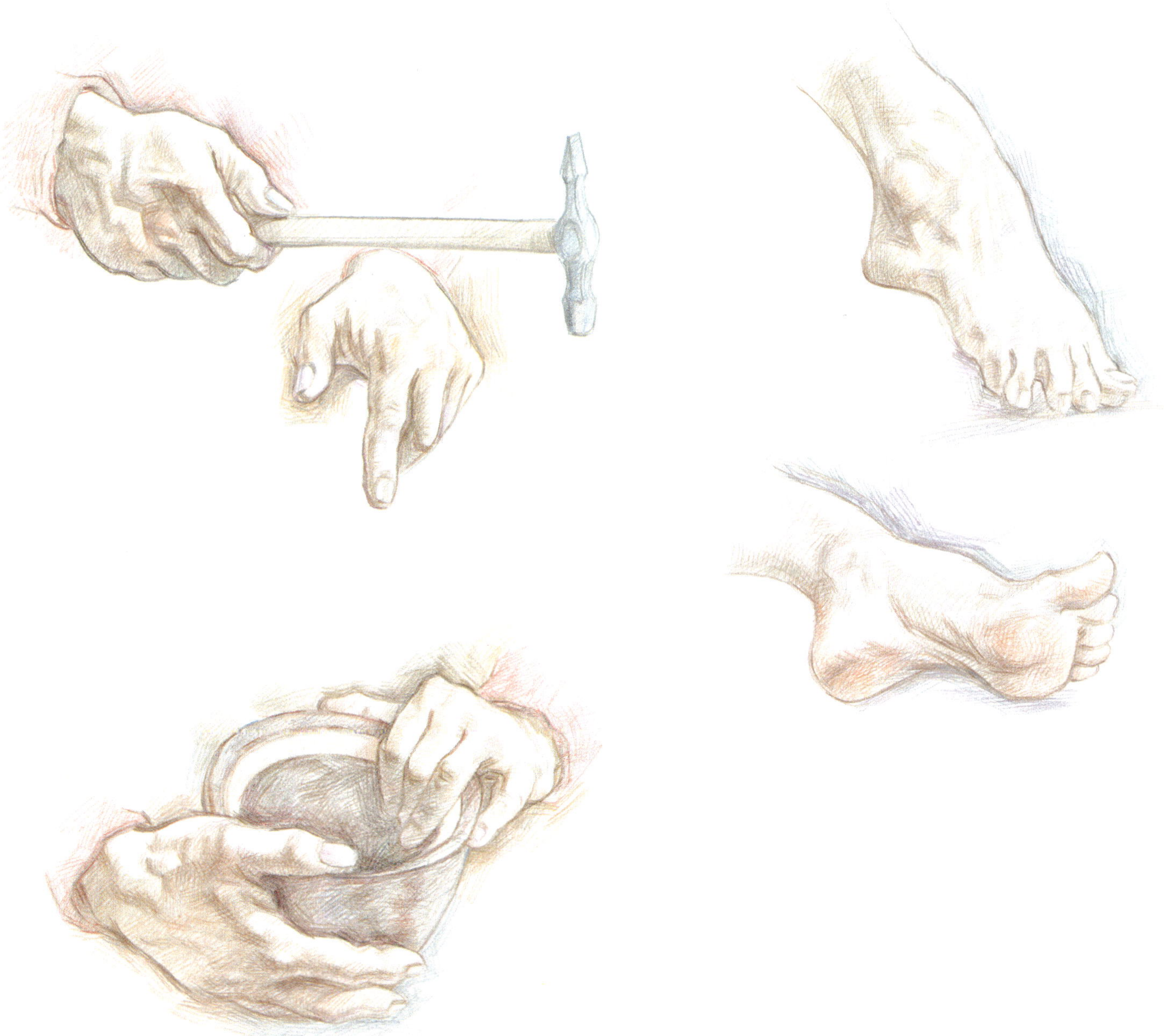

Here the model's hair also plays an important part in the shape and overall character of the head. I have often seen portrait drawings by students that appear to be no more than a mask. Little or no consideration has been given to the hair in these drawings. It's true that hair can hide vital features such as the eyes, but this is a challenge for you to meet. The hair covering this girl's face is as important to her character as the lack of hair is to the elderly man's character.

HANDS

The hands perform a vast range of movements, and seem to be in constant use. Because of this, I think that a study of hands should show them employed in some activity. Hands differ greatly from one individual to another, depending on age and occupation. With this in mind, I recommend that you practice drawing a good number of such studies. You should also vary your models as often as possible.

In the drawing at top-left, observe how the right hand gripping the hammer has well-defined veins and muscles. This creates an interesting pattern of shadow areas.

The hands holding the pot make an interesting study because of their relationship to each other in performing the task. Notice the position of the fingers relative to the thumb. On the left hand, you can see that the rim of the pot causes the little finger to adopt an unusual angle.

FEET

Feet are interesting when studied close-up. Because there is so little flesh on them, the bones and tendons are very near the surface. This means that every movement has a significant effect on the exterior form.

Drawing Movement

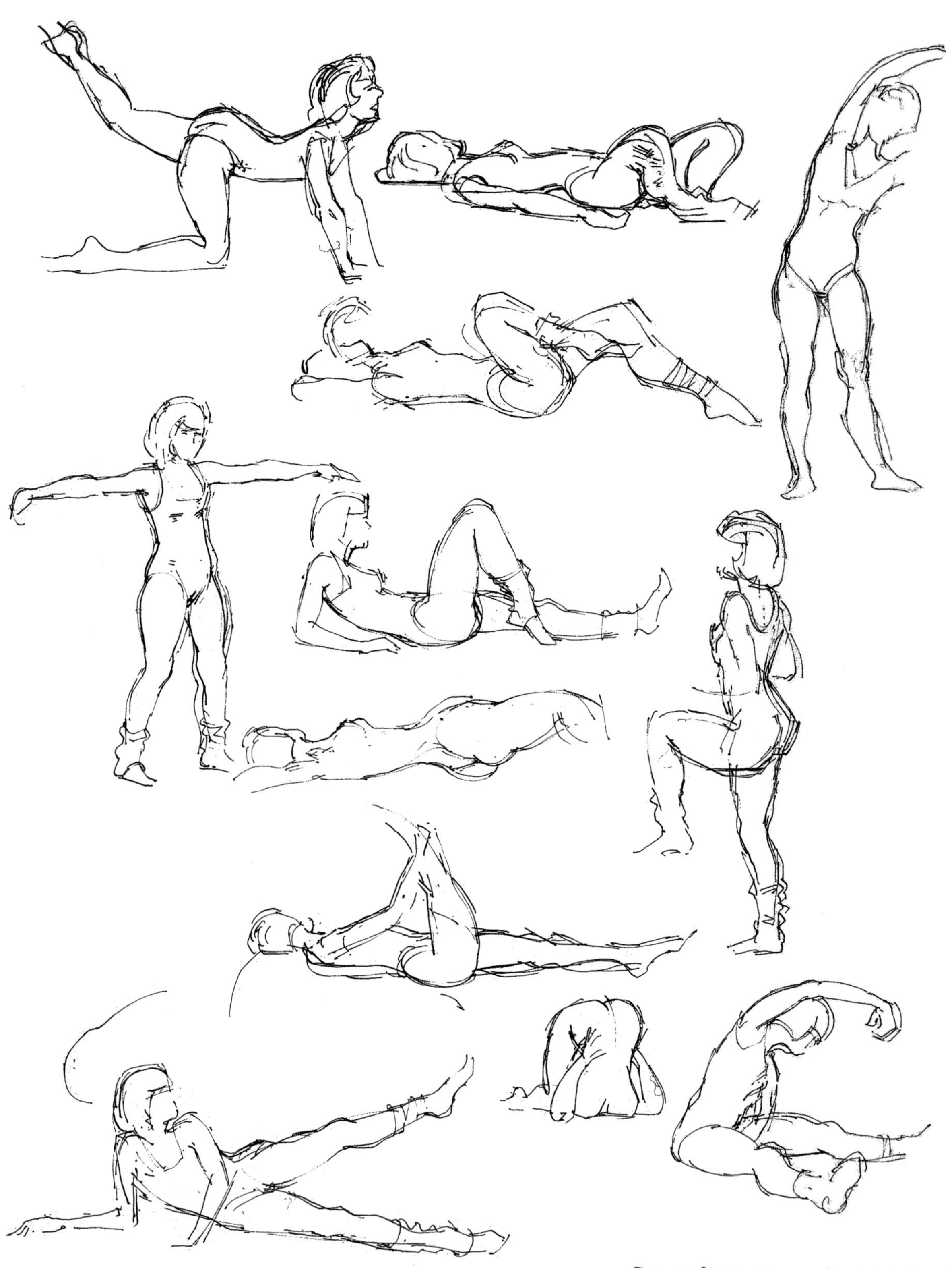

Group of one- to two-minute ink drawings made at an exercise class.

Charcoal drawing. You can make a composition like this with figures that show movement.

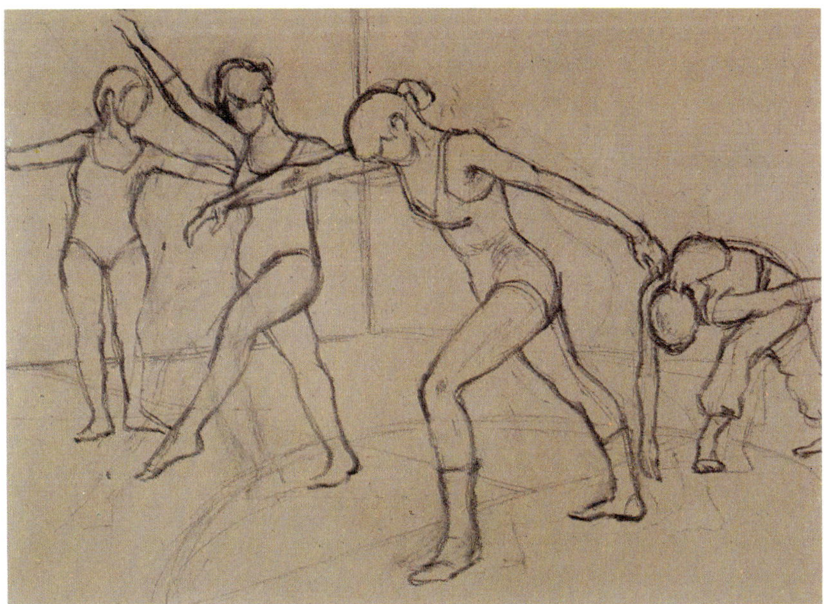

Earlier in the book I discussed the value of drawing from short poses. Poses of just a few minutes can contain expressive elements that longer poses do not. But to go one step further, where the model is not posing at all, can be very challenging.

The great value of drawing a moving figure is that you can follow a movement through from start to finish. This will help you gain a greater understanding of how the body works. When drawing from a still pose, you will look repeatedly at the model before making a mark. When drawing a moving figure such as a dancer, you will be forced to study the movement more intensely. Then you'll have to work rapidly from memory until the vision fades. You won't try to render the various parts of the body in great detail. Instead, you'll aim for a drawing that expresses the whole movement.

ON-THE-SPOT DRAWING

On the opposite page you can see a group of drawings I made at an exercise class. Each individual drawing took one to two minutes. An exercise or dance class is an ideal place to draw. The clothing worn is usually skin-tight, allowing you to observe body movements closely. Furthermore, each movement or exercise is generally repeated several times. This makes it possible for you to understand the nature of the movements in detail.

Ink is an ideal medium for movement drawing. In this case, I used a fountain pen with drawing ink. You can experiment with other media, but ink provides you with an immediate, and non-erasable, image. This is an important advantage, since the actual drawing time is so brief.

Plan to take an empty sketchbook or lots of paper with you. Once you feel at ease, you can gain momentum and produce drawings at a rapid rate. At the end of a session, it's good to lay all the drawings out on the floor. Select a few that you consider successful. You may wish to mount these on a single sheet, as I have done here.

Out of 30 or 40 drawings, you may find only five or six that work well. But don't conclude that the others are failures. Try to think of the entire group of drawings as a process that was necessary to produce those few successful ones.

COMPOSITION WITH MOVEMENT

The charcoal drawing above shows another option for working with movement. I made swift notations on the spot, then put the drawing together in the studio. My aim here was to take the movement theme a step further, into composition and design. The positions of arms and legs are vital to the flow of movement from one figure to another.

In the mixed-media drawings on the next page, I used the same idea. But I added color in the form of gouache and pastels. With the introduction of color, tone and silhouette quality are added to the purely linear method of description.

EXERCISE

Try a drawing session at a dance or exercise class. If this is not possible, have a model wear a leotard or similar outfit suitable for exercising. Then have her repeat a series of movements. Make drawings that capture the whole movement. When you have a lot of drawings, use them to make a composition, as on page 58.

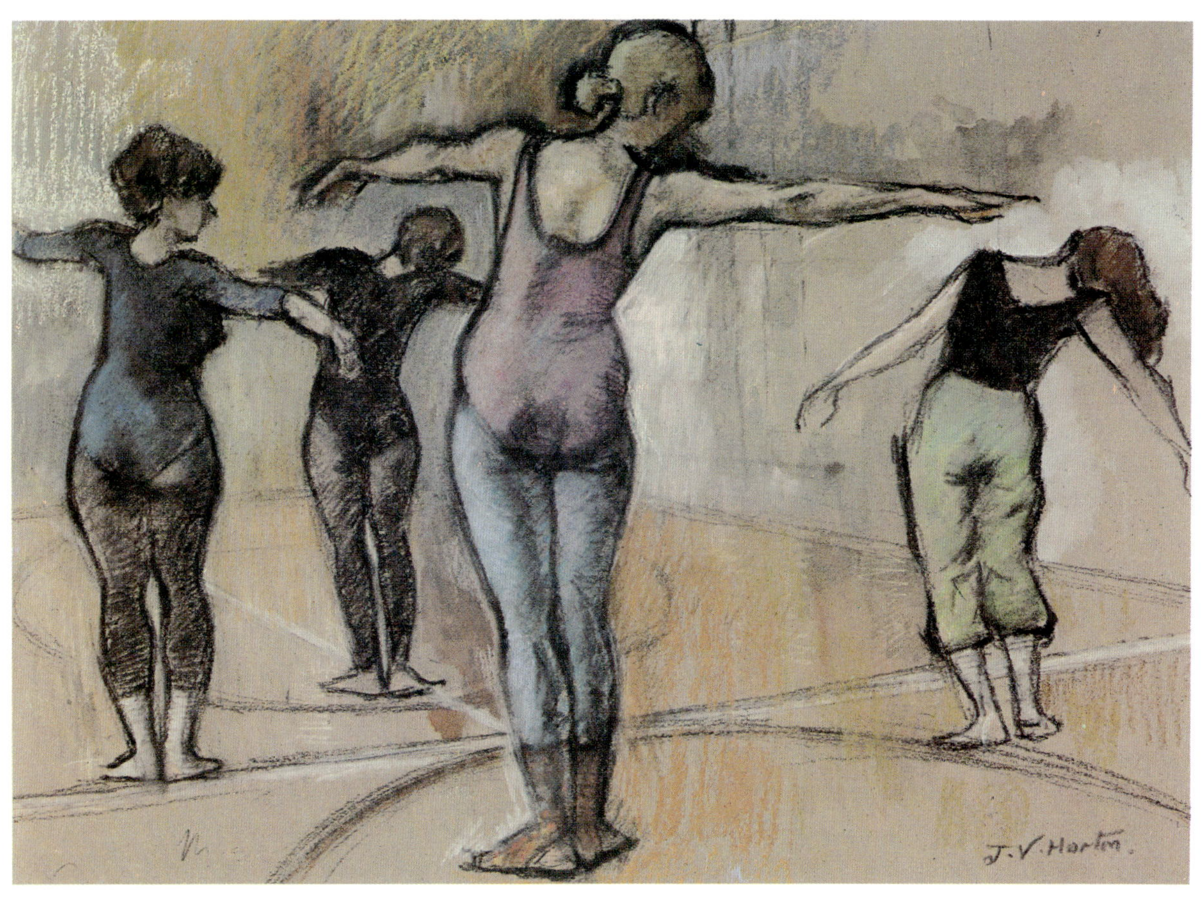

Movement drawings in charcoal, gouache and pastels.

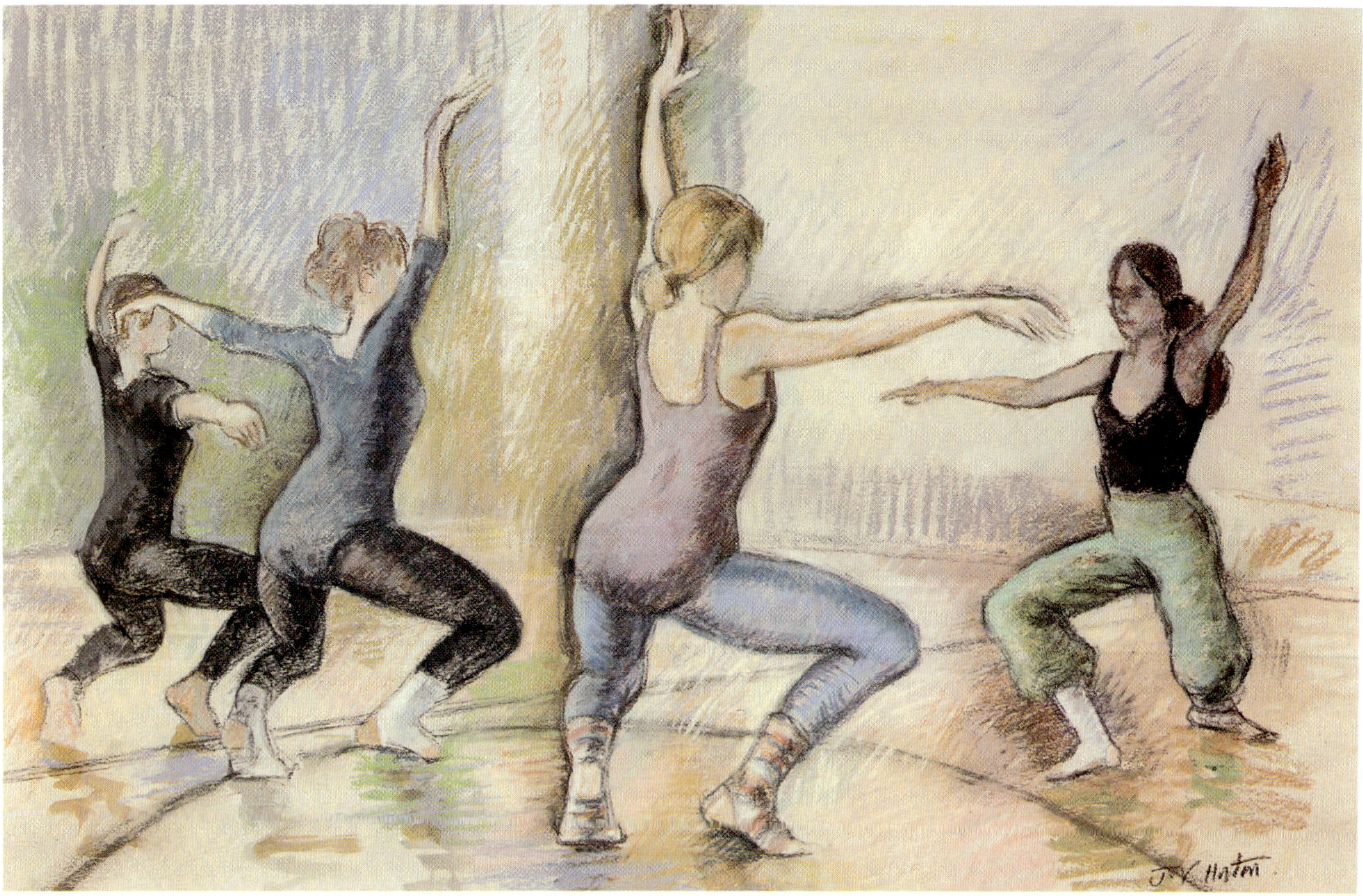

Clothed Figures

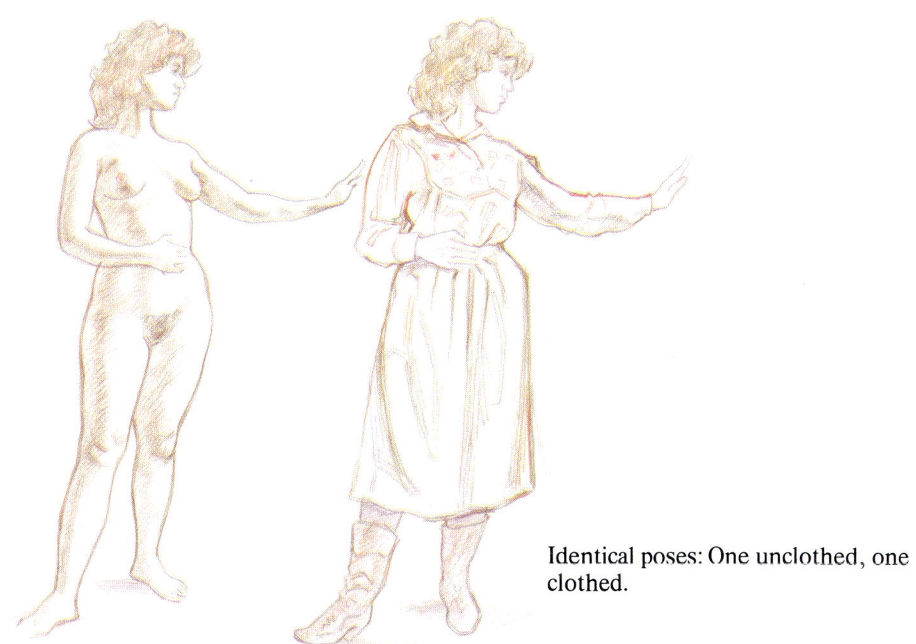

Identical poses: One unclothed, one clothed.

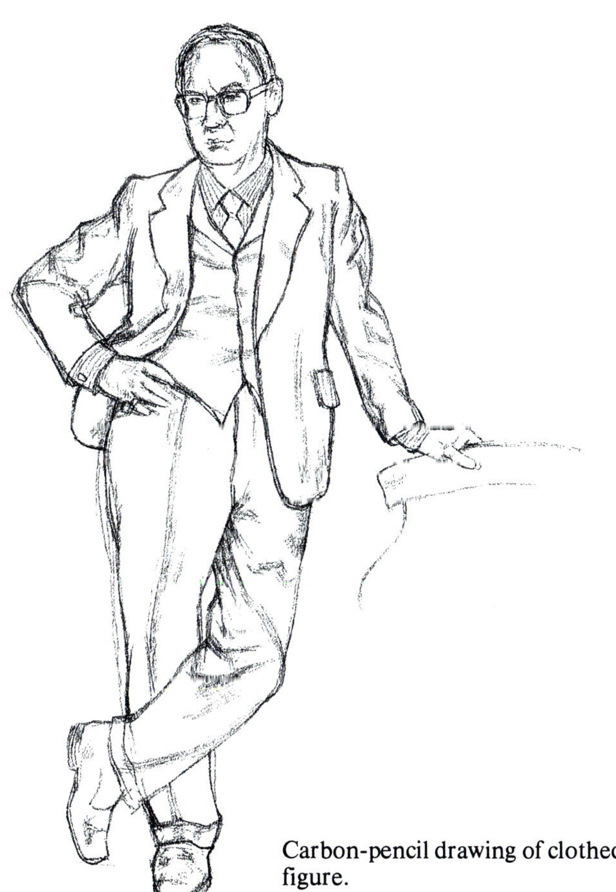

Carbon-pencil drawing of clothed figure.

I hope that the chapter on anatomy helped you to better understand the human form you see when you draw in a studio environment. In much the same way, life drawing itself will help you understand the shape of a clothed figure.

Whatever the shape of the clothing, you will always be able to observe the form underneath at certain points. This will occur wherever an article of clothing is stretched across the body. The drawings above show a figure in two identical poses—one with clothes, one without. Hips and shoulders are obvious points from which the clothes hang. Notice, too, how the sleeve is draped from the extended arm. The top edge of the arm shows the form underneath well.

I chose to make the pencil drawing below in a straightforward linear way. This approach helped me to depict the effect of folds in the suit. Where the man's limbs are bent, the clothing displays many creases. You should observe carefully the design and fit of the clothing you are drawing. A suit such as this is tailored and well-proportioned to complement the body inside.

This contrasts with the loose-fitting clothing of the figure at right on page 62. Here I was not interested in following the individual folds. Instead, I tried to capture something of the overall character of the model in her clothes.

The drawings on this page were made before a life-drawing session began. I recommend that you practice drawing your model in her clothes before beginning—or after finishing—a life drawing. This can help you understand how clothes work on a person, especially if you are already familiar with the model.

EXERCISE

Make a figure drawing from a pose of about two hours. Then ask your model to put her clothes on and resume the same pose. Make a second drawing, noting especially the stress points of the clothing. You should learn something by comparing your second drawing to your first.

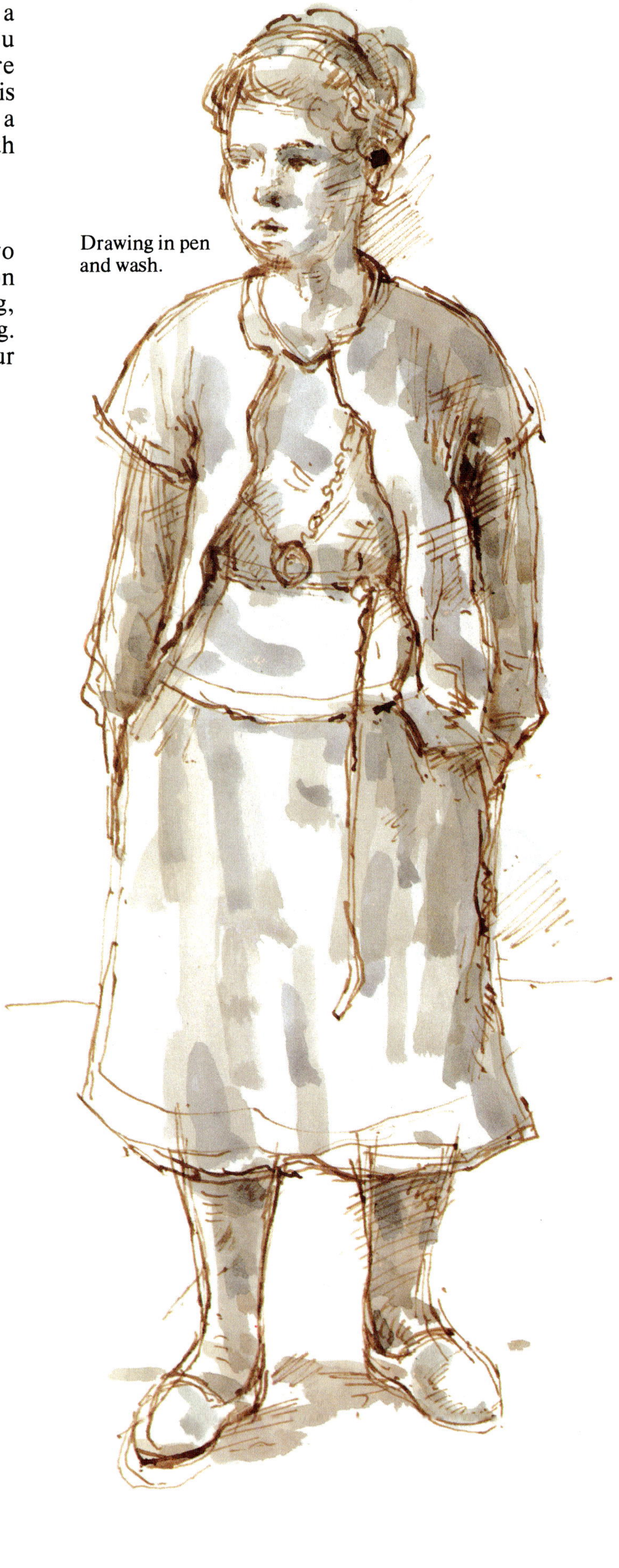

Drawing in pen and wash.

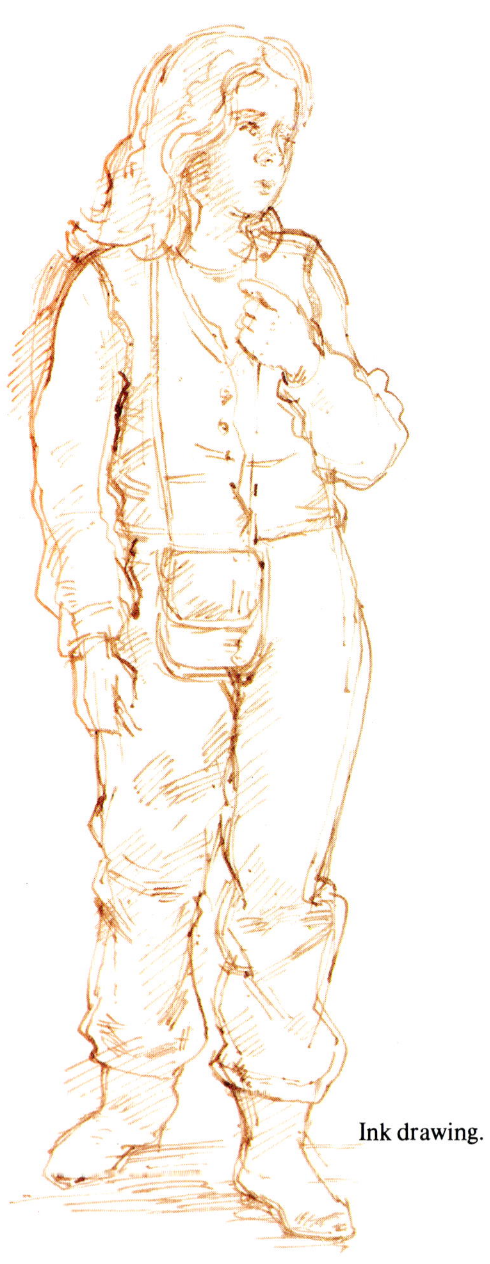

Ink drawing.

Figures In An Environment

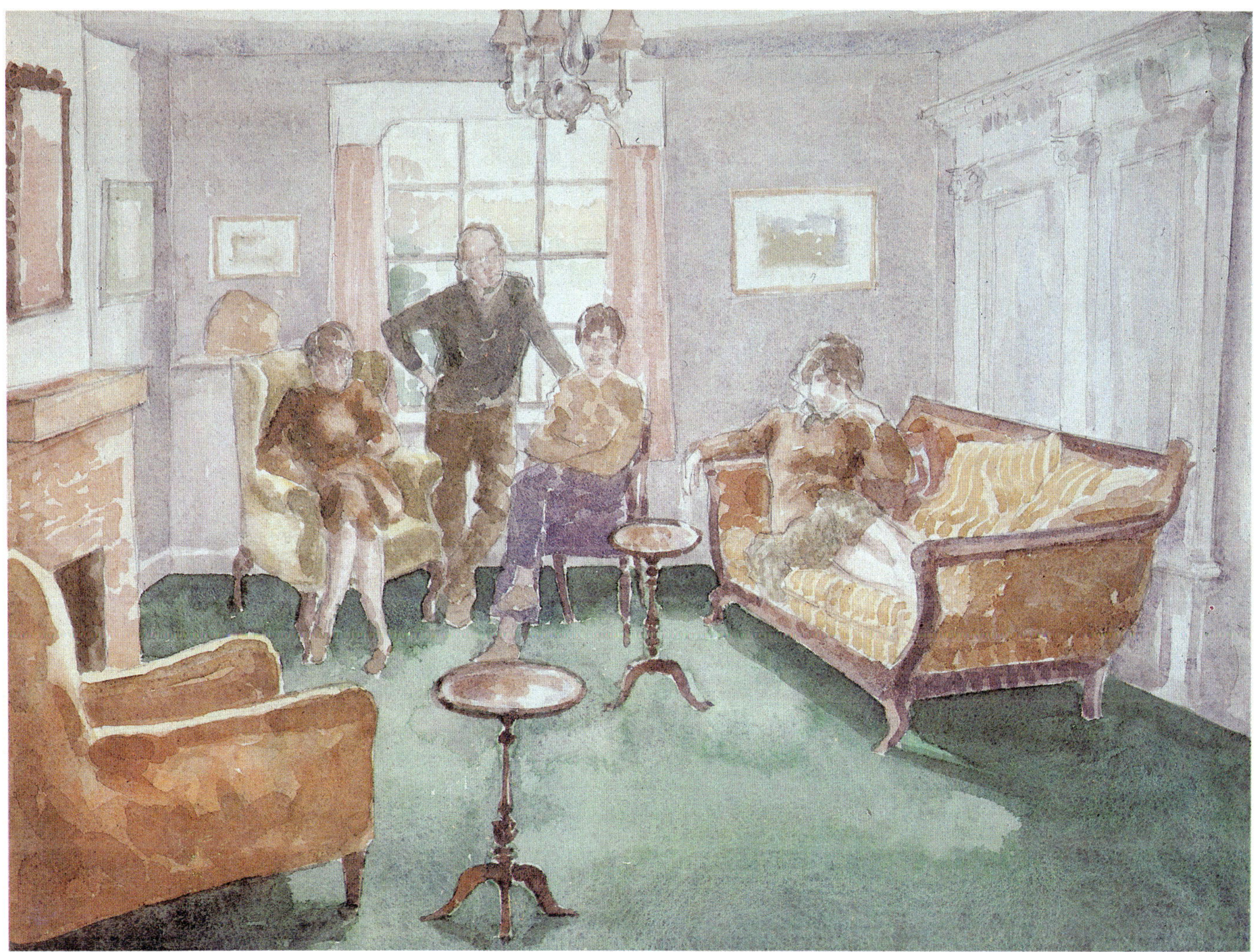

Composition in watercolor and pencil.

In this book I have been concerned mainly with single figures. When you have gained some experience with figure drawing, you are ready to progress into making a composition with several figures. You'll probably want to provide a setting for the figures too.

If you recall, I have often stressed the need to relate the figure to its immediate background. In figure drawing, this immediate background may be only a tone without any real description. But when you place several figures in an environment, a descriptive and somewhat detailed background often becomes essential. Lighting, too, is always important in creating the right background effect.

I made the above drawing as part of a series of watercolor and pencil studies. They were done in preparation for a large oil painting. I needed to experiment with the placement of these four figures in various sitting and standing poses.

When you attempt a composition of this sort, try to be particularly aware of how people behave relative to each other. Also notice if they are comfortable and relaxed, or ill at ease, in their immediate surroundings. In the composition as a whole, carefully observe the space surrounding the figures and the effect it has on them.

The watercolor drawing on page 64 shows a girl in a pose that you would typically see in a life-drawing studio. Here I chose to place her in the fairly natural surroundings of an attic bedroom. As always, the lighting was very important. I thought it essential to depict the model within the scheme of the whole interior and lighting effect. Notice how the side of her nearest the window is luminous and well-

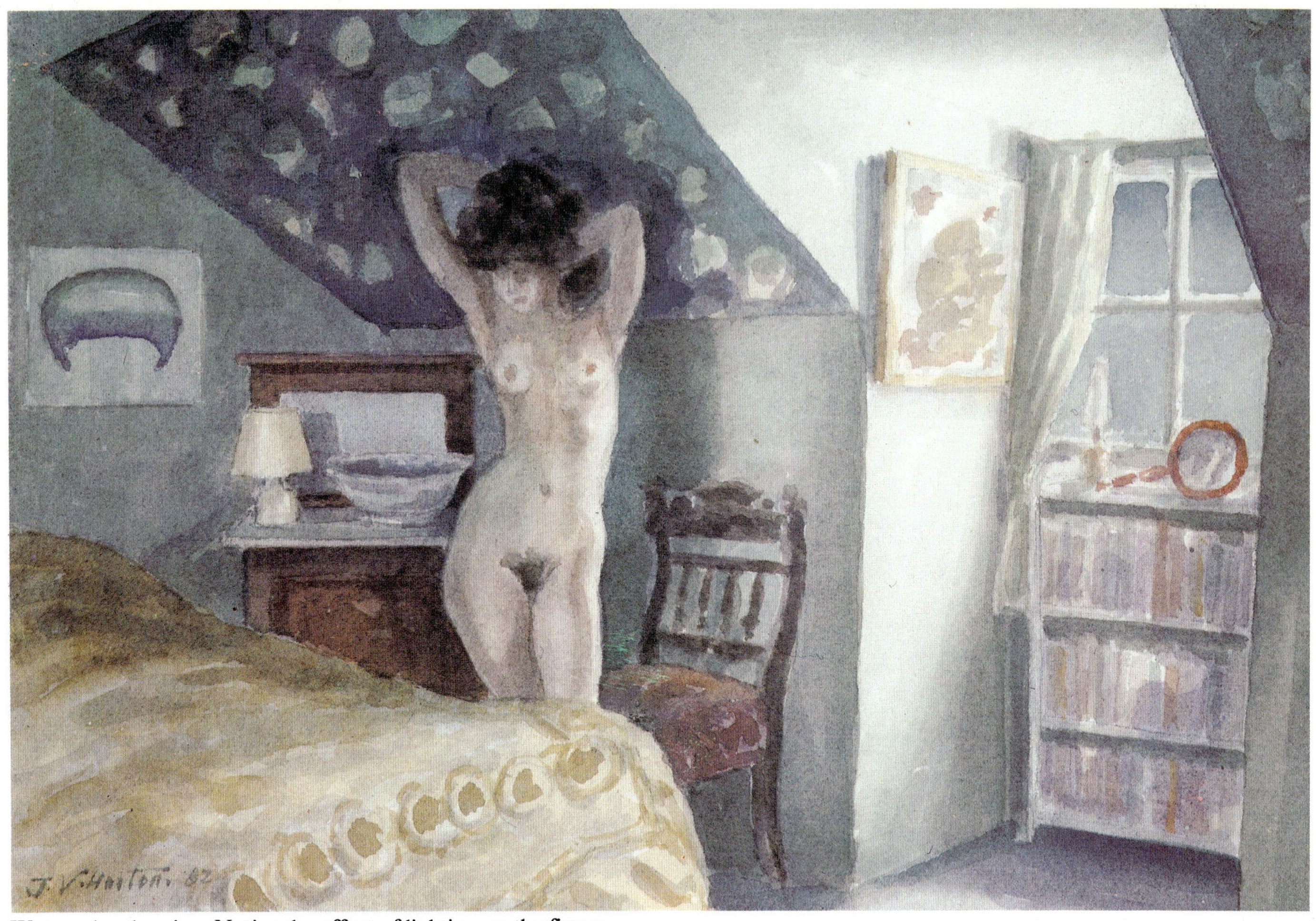

Watercolor drawing. Notice the effect of lighting on the figure.

defined. But the opposite side is much closer in tone to the background.

Because this was a vertical pose, I wanted to place the figure appropriately within the rectangle of the room. Here the figure creates a pattern with the other verticals of the window area. When you draw in similar situations, you may find yourself frustrated with the limitations of an interior. If this happens, remember to be flexible with the placement of the figure itself. Experiment with the position of your model to achieve the most proportionate and pleasing composition.